PIANO . VOCAL . GUITAR

THE ELMER BERNSTEIN
COLLECTION

Editor: Patrick Russ

Assistant Editors: Paul Henning, Jon Kull, Warren Sherk

My special thanks:
To Lisa Edmondson, for her work and care for Elmer's musical legacy.

To Emilie and Peter Bernstein, for consultation regarding the content of this collection.

To Mark Carlstein at Hal Leonard Corporation, for his careful eye to detail at every step.

To Stephen Hanson, Ned Comstock and John Brockman at the University of Southern California, for research assistance
with the Elmer Bernstein Collection at the Cinematic Arts Library.

And finally, my personal thanks and grateful appreciation to Pat Russ, for his tenacity
and devotion to the completion of this project. Thanks to him, my family and I are
confident that Elmer's lovely themes and songs will be remembered and enjoyed.

—*Eve Bernstein, October 10, 2010*

Cover photo by Robert Bruce Duncan
Used by Permission

ISBN 978-1-4234-6753-3

HAL•LEONARD®
CORPORATION
7777 W. BLUEMOUND RD. P.O. BOX 13819 MILWAUKEE, WI 53213

Visit Hal Leonard Online at
www.halleonard.com

ELMER BERNSTEIN
(1922–2004)

In a perfect cinematic world, film composers create great melodies, enhance emotions with poignant underscore, highlight action with unforgettable rhythmic drive, and pen songs that stand the test of time. Success in any of these elements ensures a good score, but one composer did it all and made it look easy: Elmer Bernstein. Bernstein composed timeless themes for classic films in a career that encompassed more than 200 scores. He received Academy Award® nominations in six consecutive decades—still a record—garnering fourteen nominations, and winning best Music Score for the film version of the musical *Thoroughly Modern Millie.*

Elmer began his professional musical life as a critically acclaimed concert pianist, but found that performing the same program over and over on tour was not artistically satisfying. One of his earliest personal struggles involved his decision to stop concertizing in favor of a more creative outlet: composing. To give up his developing concert career in favor of an unknown future required a leap of faith, but he never looked back. When a new acquaintance would ask him what he did for a living, Elmer responded simply, "I am a composer." He loved his profession, and he wrote for every occasion: film, theater, musicals, television, tributes, charities, dedications, personal gifts and just for the simple joy of creating. Over the years he said that he wanted to continue composing to the very end, which in fact he did, premiering his last orchestral piece *Fanfare for the Hollywood Bowl* just ten weeks before he died of cancer at age 82.

Elmer demonstrated his new film themes on piano for directors, his assistants, and family. The first time he met with his orchestrator on a new project, Elmer would often take a seat at the piano and say, "The tune goes something like this..." What followed was an exquisite piano setting which perfectly captured the essence of his score. His ability to translate a large work into a smaller setting without losing any of the piece's character was vintage Elmer Bernstein. It is also the reason that the selections in this folio work so well in their piano and vocal settings. Many of these arrangements were created or edited by Elmer Bernstein himself, even though he didn't place an arranger credit on the original published versions. I've left them as he did, only distinguishing when I or another person created a setting that you find in this volume.

One piece in this folio occurs in two settings. *To Kill a Mockingbird* has a lovely adaptation by Roy Phillippe, which Elmer went over and changed very little. The other setting Elmer made himself as a gift to his daughter Emilie on the occasion of her tenth birthday. He said that he wrote *Mockingbird* from a child's point of view, and it seems appropriate to include his own setting intended for children to play. Elmer enjoyed children, responding to any child's request with kindness and affection, and helped many young people (including me) on their career paths.

Elmer knew his own worth as a composer, yet was genuinely modest about his own achievements. He felt that if he could lift someone's spirits just for an hour, he had done his job. Once, he and his wife Eve were visiting the small town of La Bisbal, near Barcelona, Spain, in the intense summer heat. They pulled over in the small village plaza and ordered a cool drink on the café veranda. A little boy on the porch inserted a coin in a mechanical horse ride, which bounced jauntily to the strains of *The Magnificent Seven*. Elmer realized that if his music played even a small part in people's everyday lives, his efforts had made a difference. After reading through this volume of best-loved music, no doubt you will agree.

Patrick Russ
Symphonic Orchestrator

A complete list of Elmer Bernstein's many compositions and awards can be found on his official website: **www.elmerbernstein.com**. His collected works are available for study in the Cinematic Arts Library at the University of Southern California.

CONTENTS

THE AGE OF INNOCENCE
from the 1993 Film THE AGE OF INNOCENCE

By ELMER BERNSTEIN
Piano arrangement by Patrick Russ

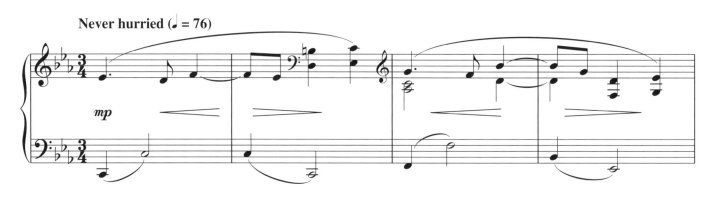

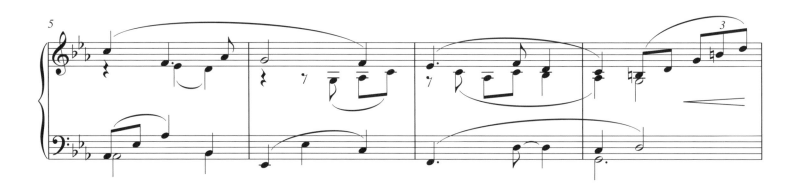

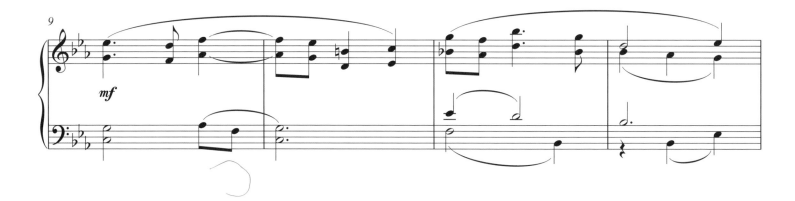

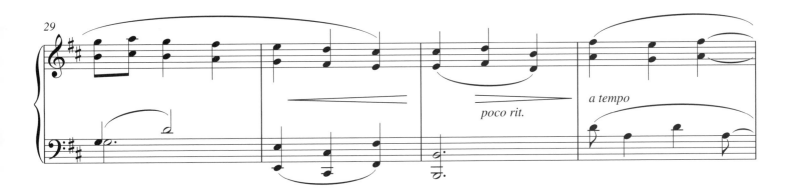

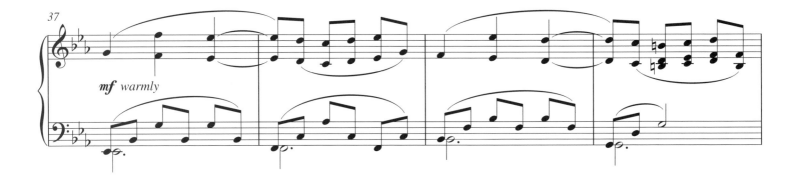

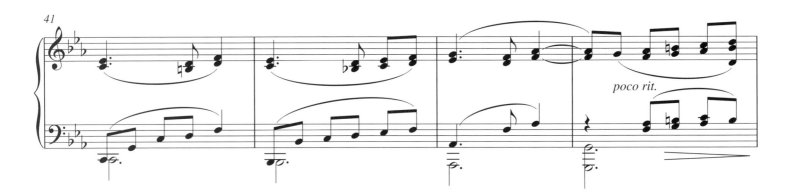

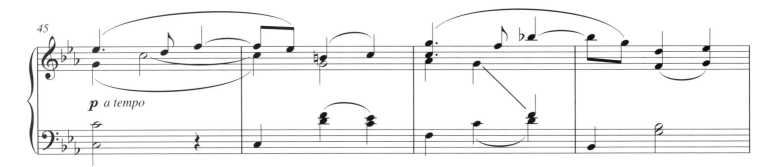

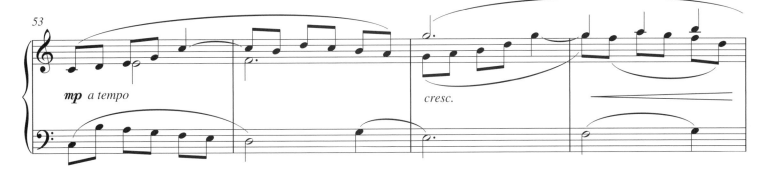

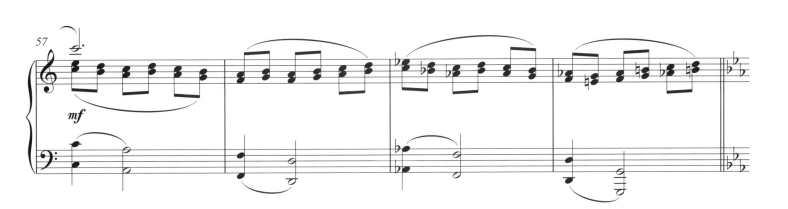

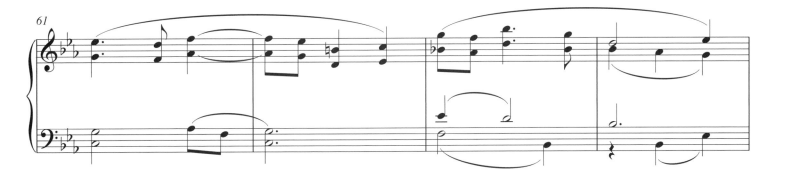

ANIMAL HOUSE
(Faber College Theme)
from the 1978 Film ANIMAL HOUSE

By ELMER BERNSTEIN
Piano arrangement by Patrick Russ

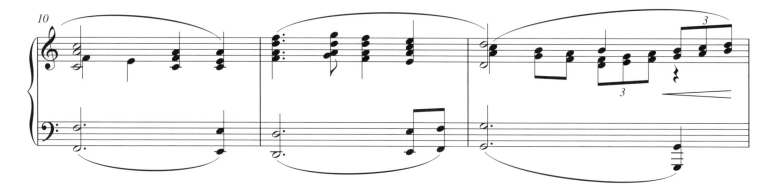

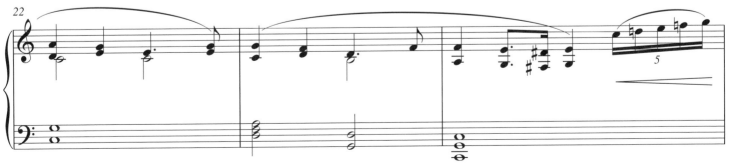

* Based on a Bosnian folksong

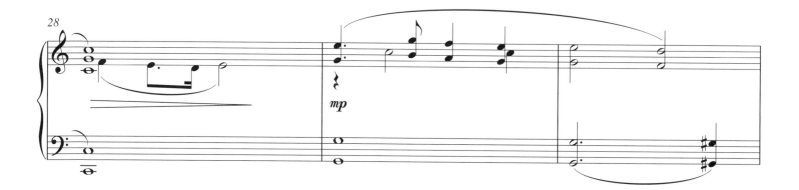

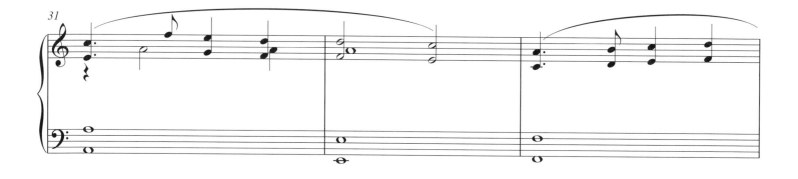

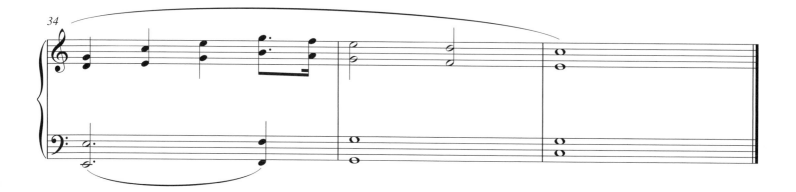

ARE YOU READY FOR THE SUMMER?

from the 1979 Film MEATBALLS

Words by NORMAN GIMBEL
Music by ELMER BERNSTEIN

Moderately fast (♩ = 154)

Are you read-y for the sum-mer? _____

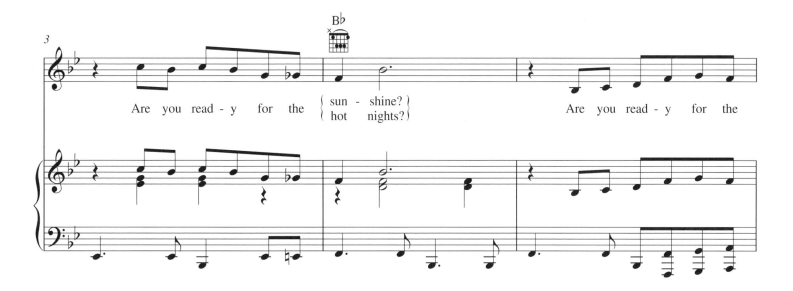

Are you read-y for the {sun - shine? / hot nights?} Are you read-y for the

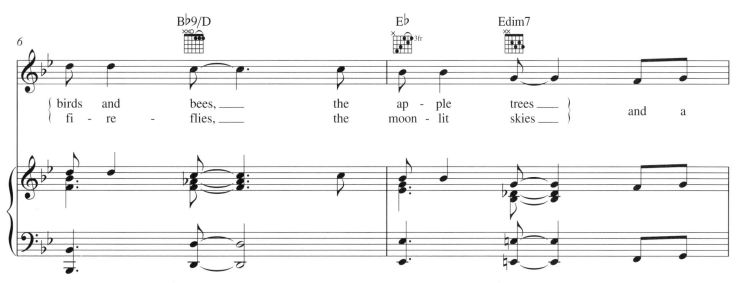

{birds and bees, _____ the ap-ple trees _____ / fi - re - flies, _____ the moon - lit skies _____} and a

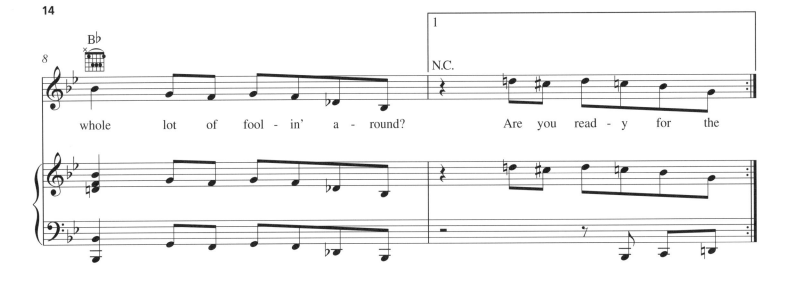

whole lot of fool - in' a - round? Are you read - y for the

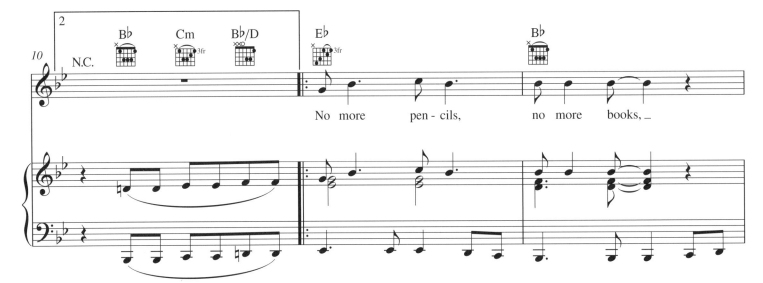

No more pen - cils, no more books, __

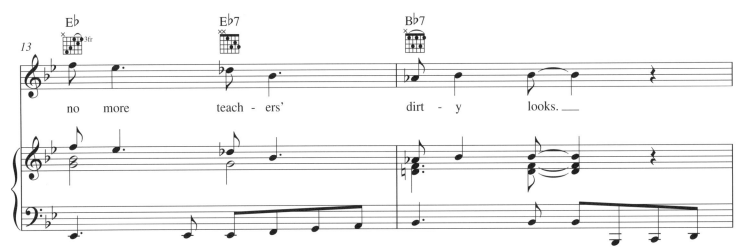

no more teach - ers' dirt - y looks. __

No more math __ and his - to - ry, __ sum - mer time __ has

THEME FROM
"BABY THE RAIN MUST FALL"

(1965)

Words and Music by ELMER BERNSTEIN
and ERNIE SHELDON

Moving and steady ($\quarternote$ =110)

Some men climb a moun - tain.
do not love for sil - ver.
am not rich or fa - mous,
Some men swim the sea.
Do not love for gold.
but who can ev - er tell.
My
I

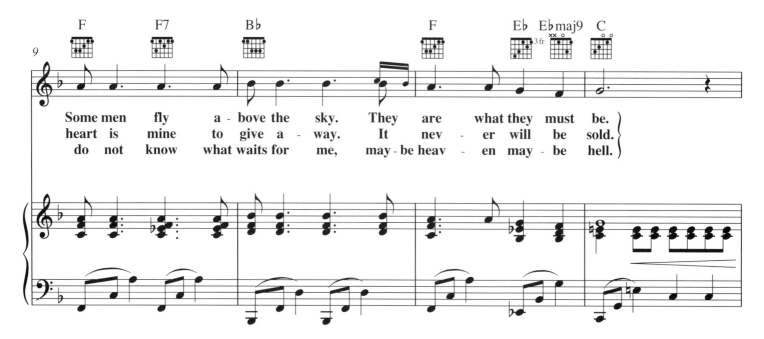

Some men fly a - bove the sky. They are what they must be.
heart is mine to give a - way. It nev - er will be sold.
do not know what waits for me, may - be heav - en may - be hell.

THE BUCCANEER - LOVE SONG
(Lovers' Gold)
from the 1958 Film THE BUCCANEER

Words by MACK DAVID
Music by ELMER BERNSTEIN

DELILAH JONES
from the 1955 Film THE MAN WITH THE GOLDEN ARM

Words by SYLVIA FINE
Music by ELMER BERNSTEIN

THEME FROM BY LOVE POSSESSED

from the 1961 Film BY LOVE POSSESSED

Words by SAMMY CAHN
Music by ELMER BERNSTEIN

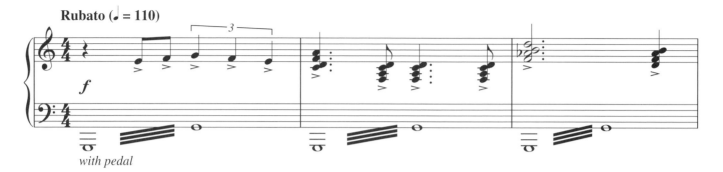

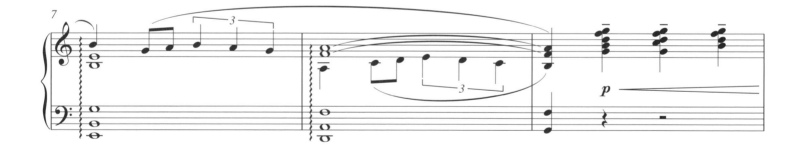

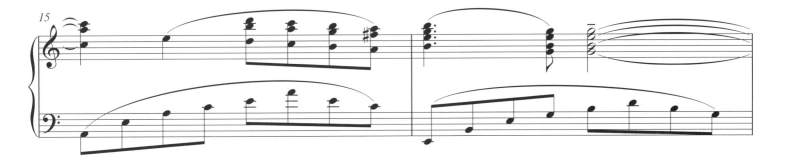

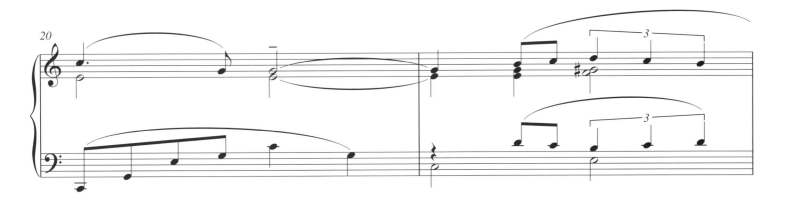

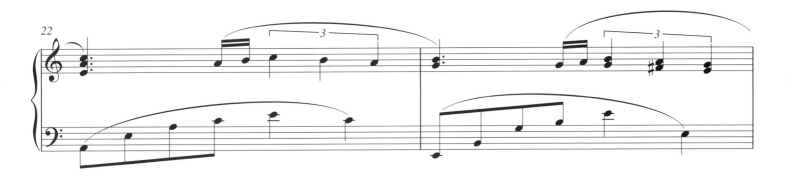

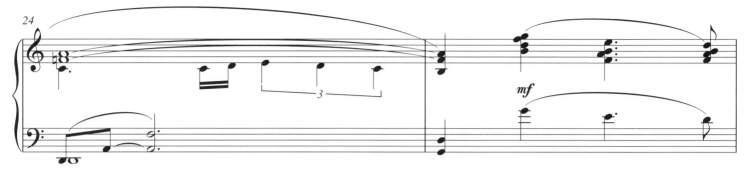

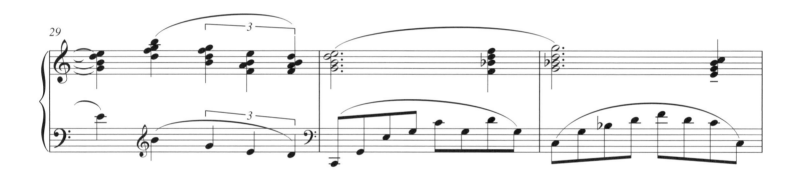

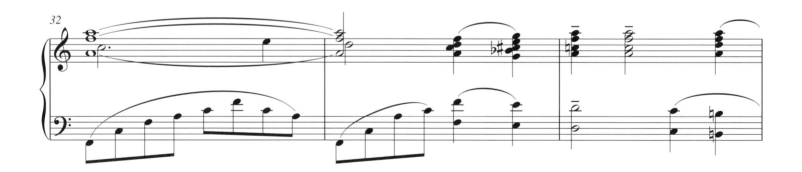

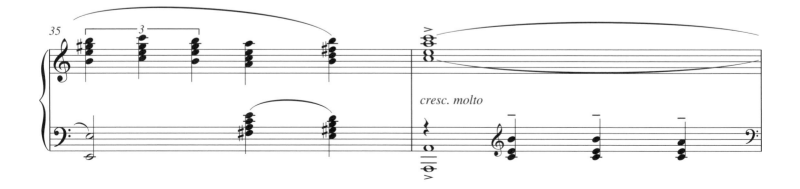

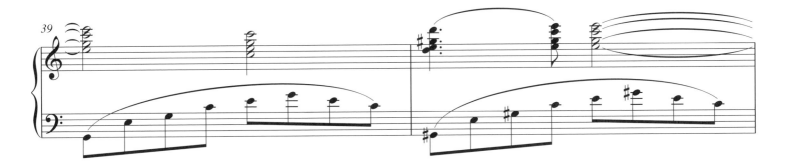

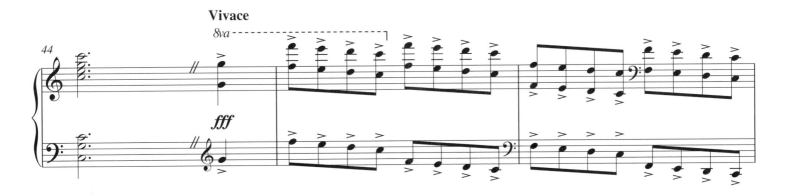

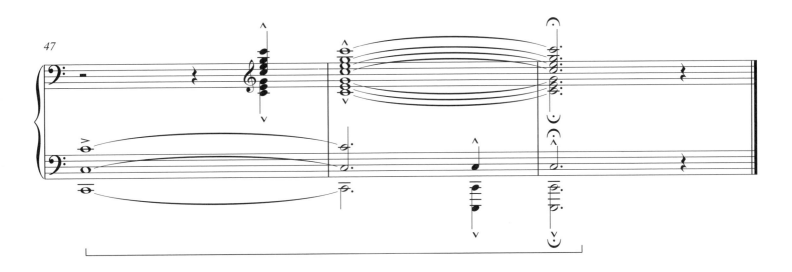

THEME FROM BY LOVE POSSESSED

from the 1961 Film BY LOVE POSSESSED

Words by SAMMY CAHN
Music by ELMER BERNSTEIN

DESIRE UNDER THE ELMS

Love Theme from the 1958 Film DESIRE UNDER THE ELMS

By ELMER BERNSTEIN

Moderately slow, with expression (♩ = 60)

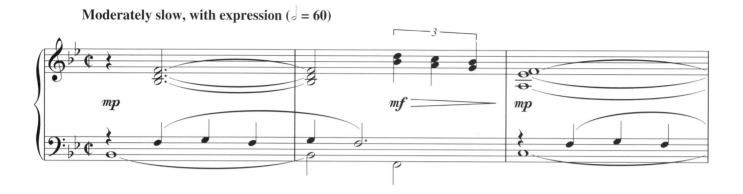

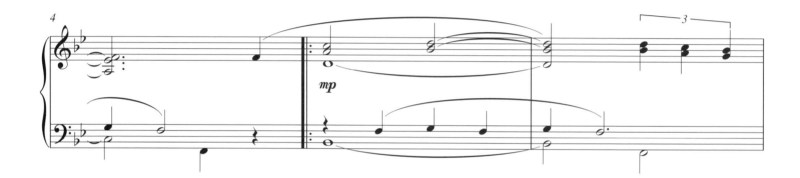

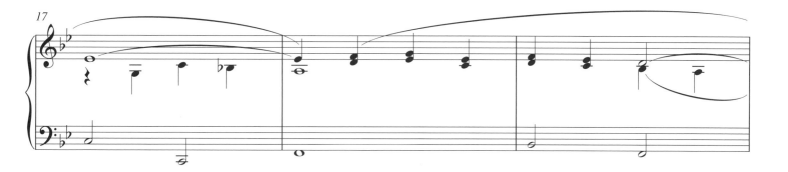

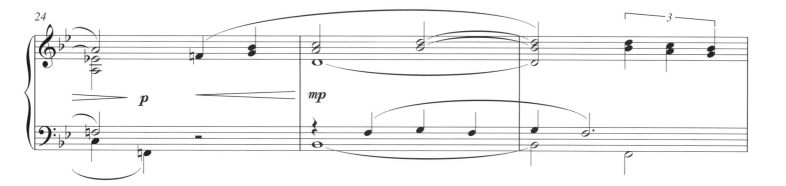

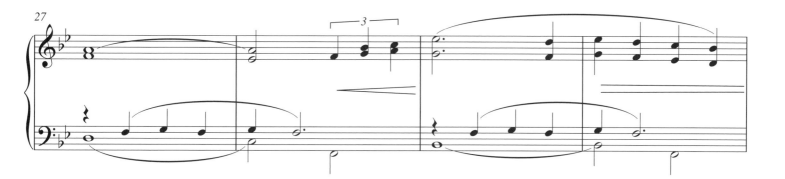

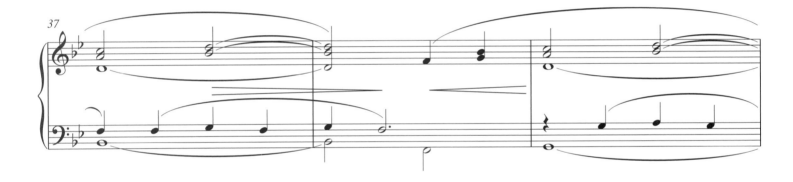

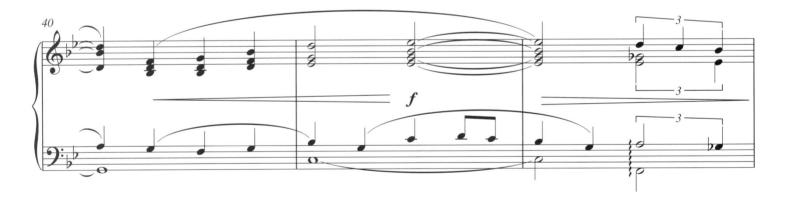

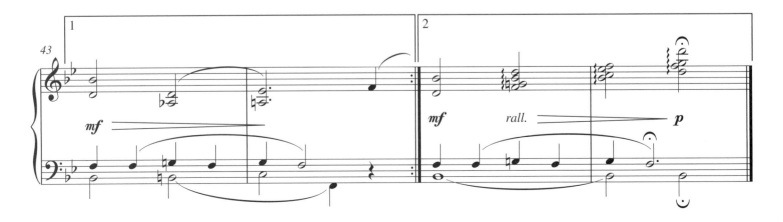

FAR FROM HEAVEN

from the 2002 Film FAR FROM HEAVEN

By ELMER BERNSTEIN
Piano arrangement by Elmer Bernstein

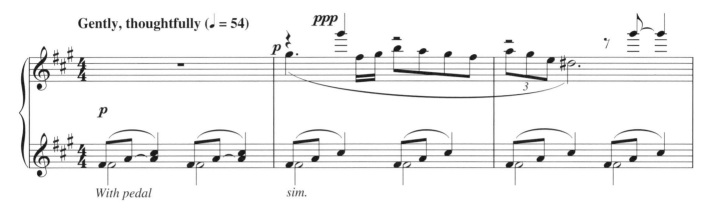

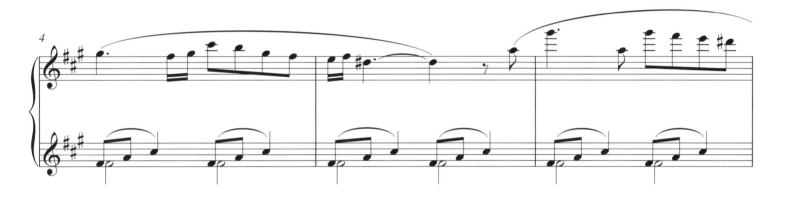

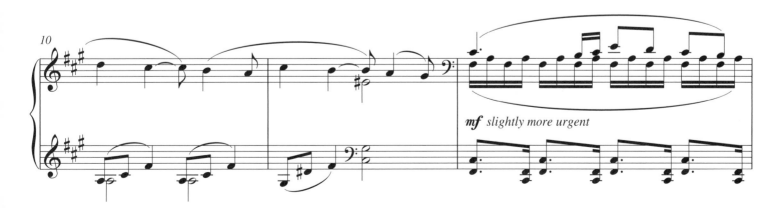

passionate again

winding down, taking time

slowing

p forever

January 1, 2003

THEME FROM ELLERY QUEEN
from the TV Series ELLERY QUEEN
(1975)

By ELMER BERNSTEIN

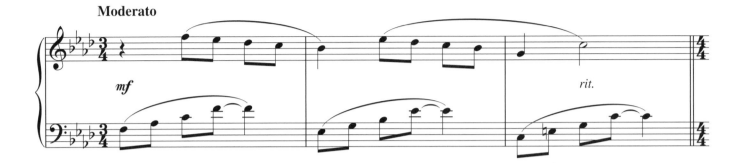

FROM MY WINDOW

from the 1995 Film FRANKIE STARLIGHT

Words by EMILIE A. BERNSTEIN
Music by ELMER BERNSTEIN

A GIRL NAMED TAMIKO

from the 1962 Motion Picture A GIRL NAMED TAMIKO

Words by MACK DAVID
Music by ELMER BERNSTEIN

Moderately slow, expressively (♩ = 112)

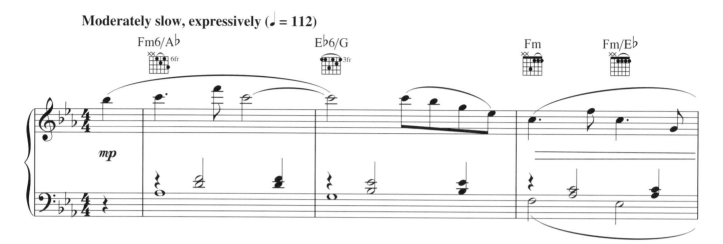

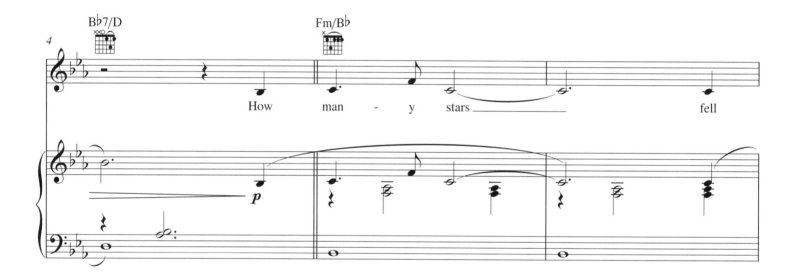

How man - y stars _____ fell

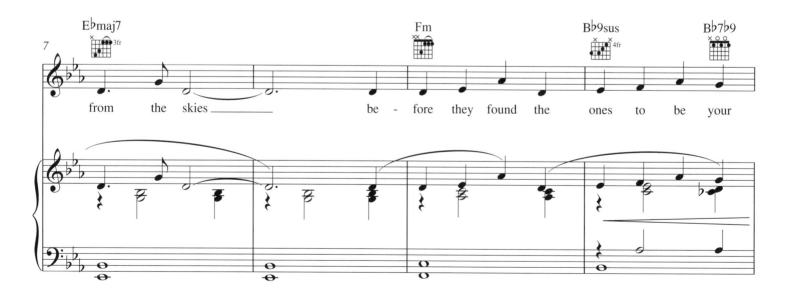

from the skies _____ be - fore they found the ones to be your

Ta - mi - ko, _____ Ta -

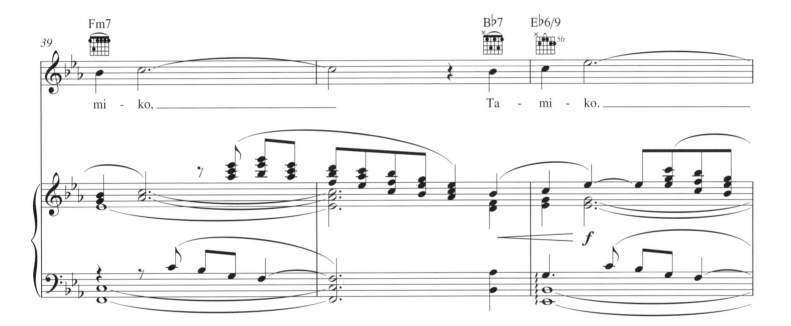

mi - ko, _____ Ta - mi - ko. _____

THE GREAT ESCAPE MARCH
from the 1963 Film THE GREAT ESCAPE

Words by AL STILLMAN
Music by ELMER BERNSTEIN
Piano arrangement by Patrick Russ

THE GRIFTERS
from the 1990 Film THE GRIFTERS

By ELMER BERNSTEIN
Piano arrangement by Patrick Russ

With steady intent (♩ = 120)

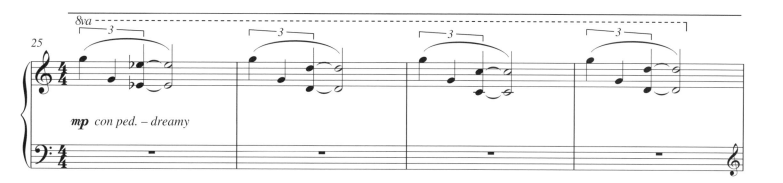

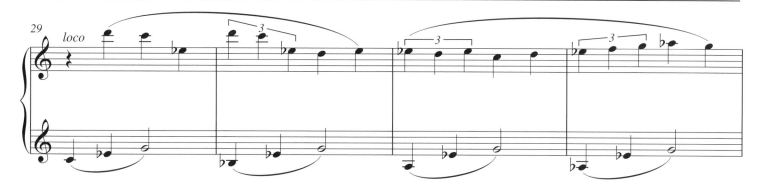

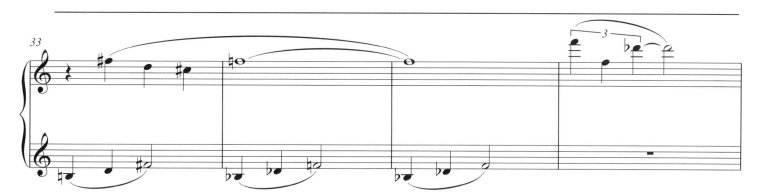

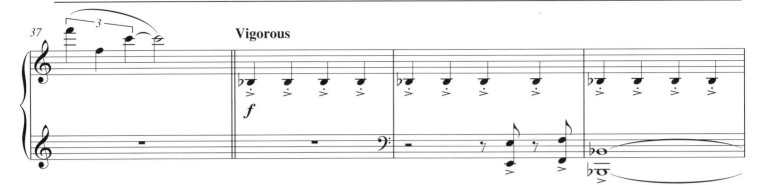

Vigorous

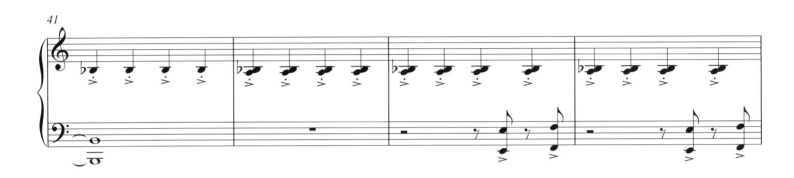

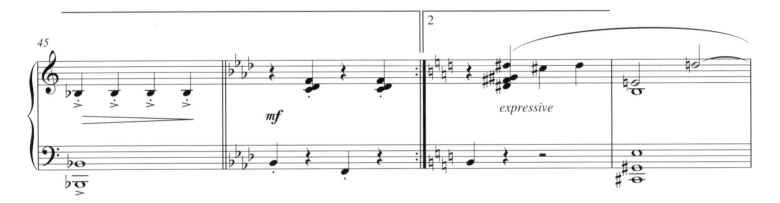

THE HALLELUJAH TRAIL
(Main Theme)
from the 1965 Film THE HALLELUJAH TRAIL

Words by ERNIE SHELDON
Music by ELMER BERNSTEIN
Arranged by Patrick Russ

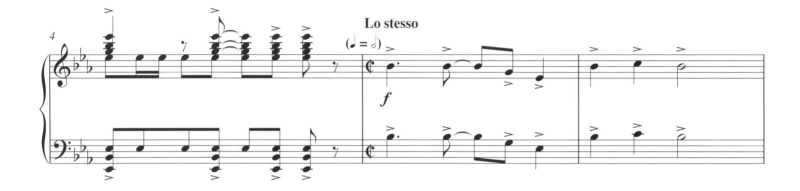

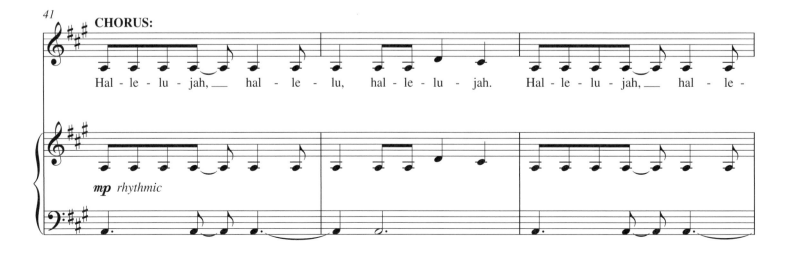

Hal - le - lu - jah, ___ hal - le - lu, hal - le - lu - jah. Hal - le - lu - jah, ___ hal - le -

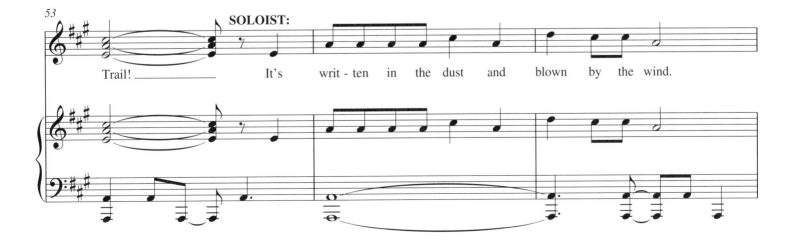

Hal - le - lu - jah Trail! Hal - le -

lu - jah, ___ hal - le - lu - jah, ___ hal - le -

lu - jah, ___ hal - le - lu, Hal - le - lu - jah Trail!

SOLOIST: Ear - ly in the morn - in', al - most day. **CHORUS:** Hal - le - lu - jah

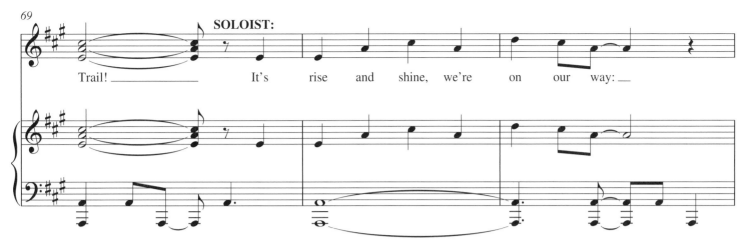

lu - jah, ___ hal - le - lu - jah, ___ hal - le -

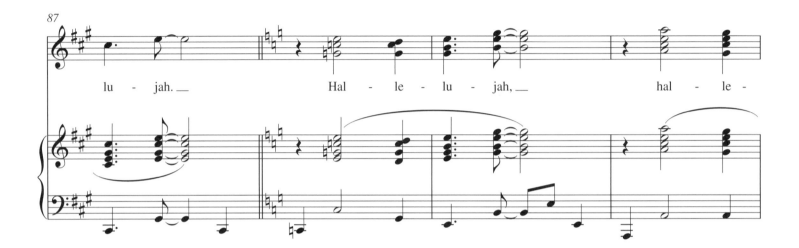

lu - jah. ___ Hal - le - lu - jah, ___ hal - le -

lu - jah, ___ hal - le - lu - jah, _____ hal - le -

Broaden

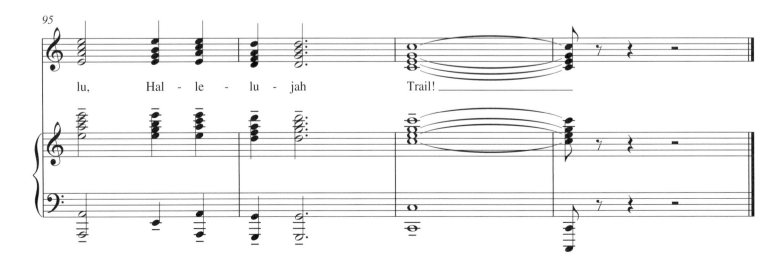

lu, Hal - le - lu - jah Trail! _____

HAWAII
(Main Theme)
from the 1966 Film HAWAII

Words by MACK DAVID
Music by ELMER BERNSTEIN

rain wash your cares far out to sea.

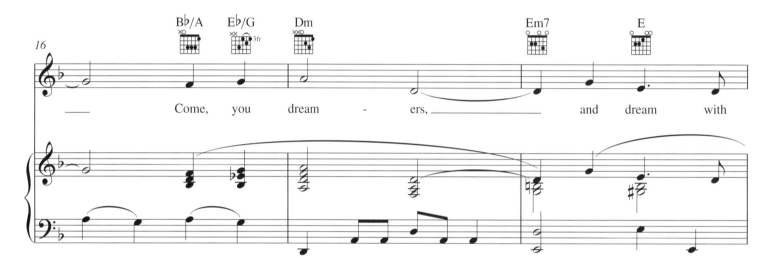

Come, you dream - ers, and dream with

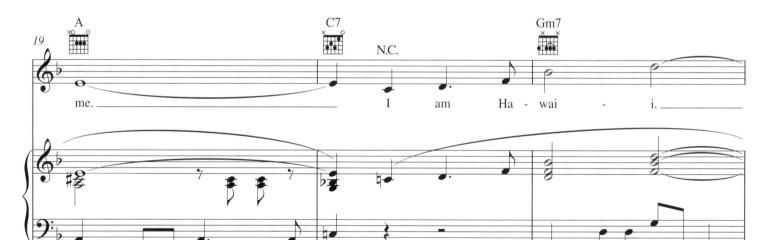

me. I am Ha-wai - i.

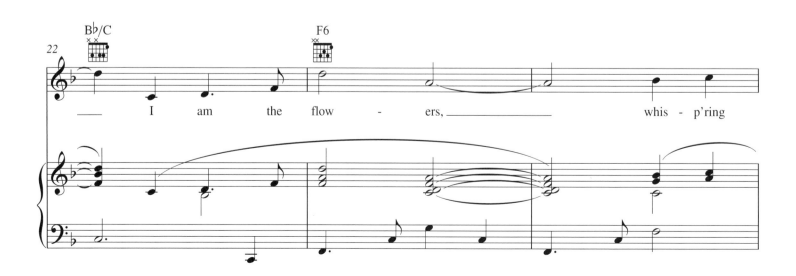

I am the flow - ers, whis - p'ring

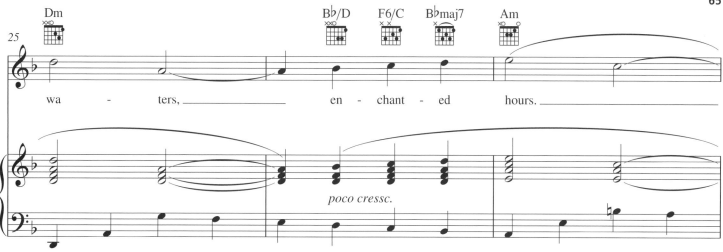

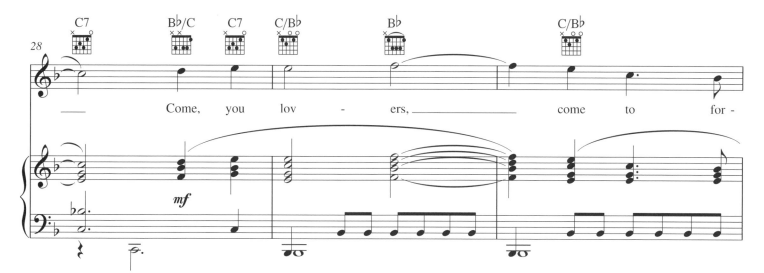

HEAVY METAL
from the 1981 Film HEAVY METAL

By ELMER BERNSTEIN
Piano arrangement by Patrick Russ

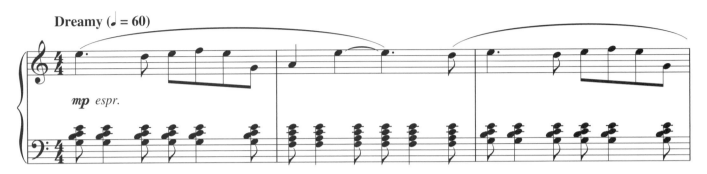

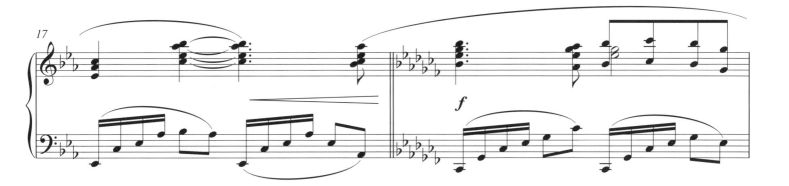

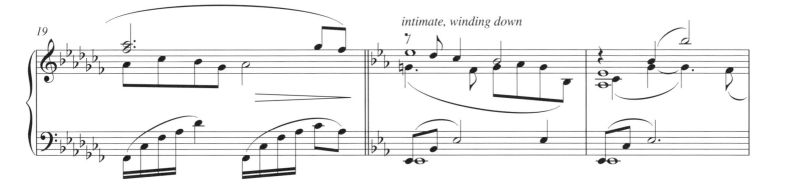

HELLO & GOODBYE

from the 1976 Film FROM NOON TILL THREE

Words by ALAN and MARILYN BERGMAN
Music by ELMER BERNSTEIN

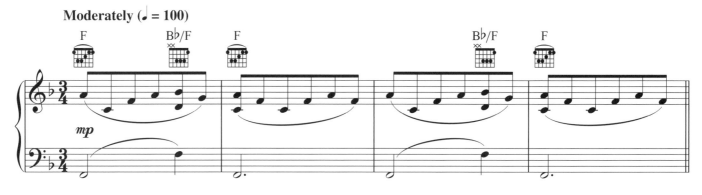

Some have a life-time, some just a day.
mu-sic has end-ed, I still just hear the song. ___ Our

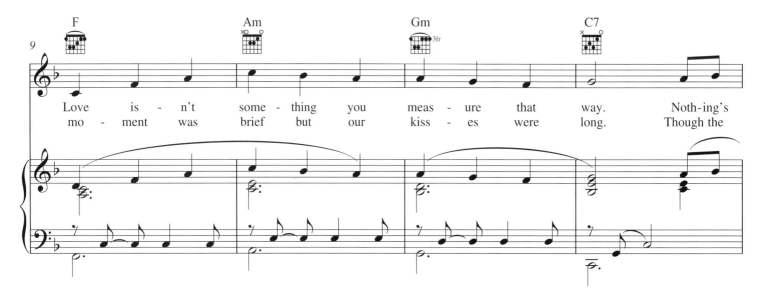

Love is-n't some-thing you meas-ure that way. Noth-ing's
mo-ment was brief but our kiss-es were long. Though the

70

HUD

from the 1963 Film HUD

Words by MACK DAVID
Music by ELMER BERNSTEIN

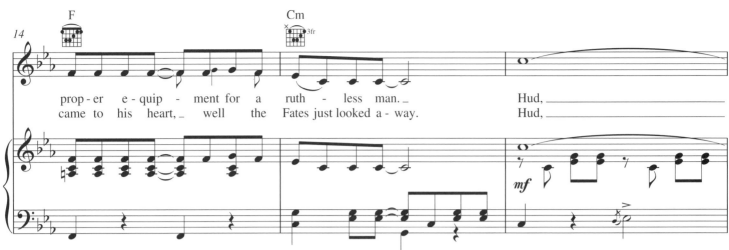

prop - er e - quip - ment for a ruth - less man.
came to his heart, _ well the Fates just looked a - way.

Hud, _____
Hud, _____

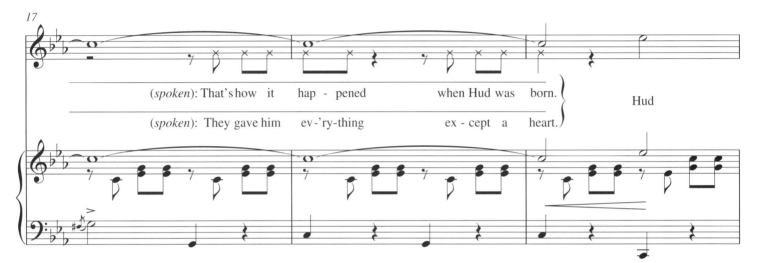

(spoken): That's how it hap - pened when Hud was born.

(spoken): They gave him ev -'ry-thing ex - cept a heart.

Hud

Ban - non. _____

Hud, _____

Hud _ Ban - non. _____

His

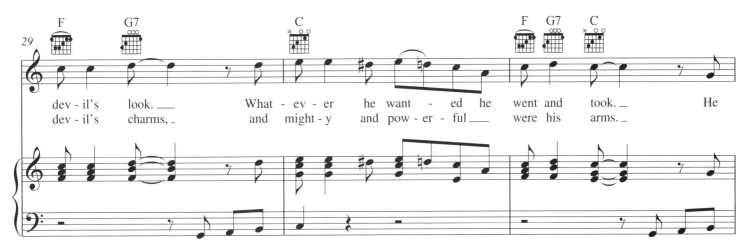

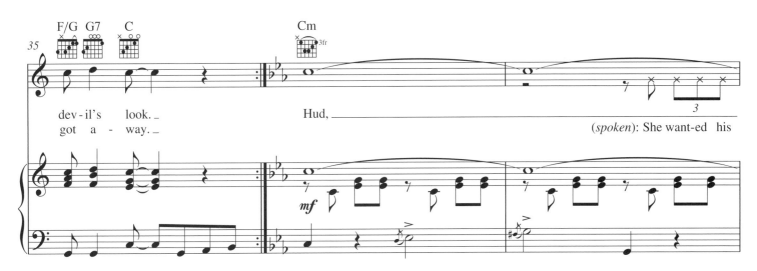

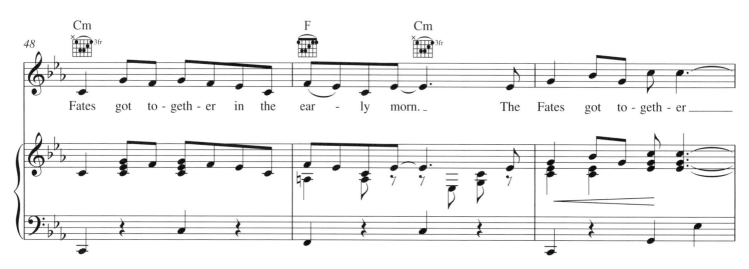

and they

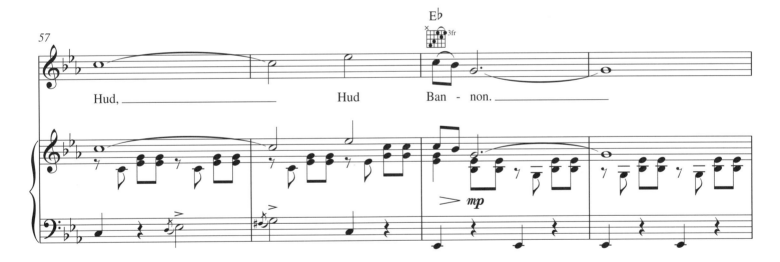

made a ___ man un-a-ble to love. ___ They made a lone - ly man. ___

Hud, ___ Hud Ban - non. ___

Hud, ___ Hud ___ Ban - non. ___

I LOVE YOU, ALICE B. TOKLAS

from the 1968 Film I LOVE YOU, ALICE B. TOKLAS

Words by PAUL MAZURSKY
and LARRY TUCKER
Music by ELMER BERNSTEIN

Red vel - vet trees and li - ons, grin - ning li - ons, can - dy witch - es eat - ing
Green wool - ly gold - en gar - dens, Mar - vin Gar - dens, co - ri - an - der, ba - by

li - tchi leaves, spin - ning rain - bow - ing light.
el - e - phants sing - ing "Si - lent

Night."

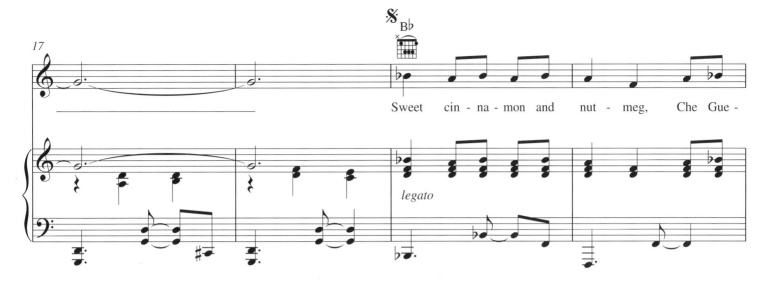

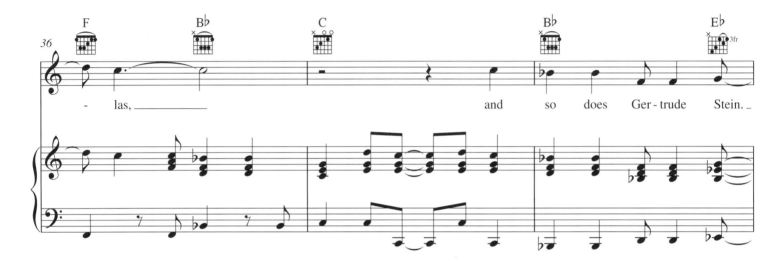

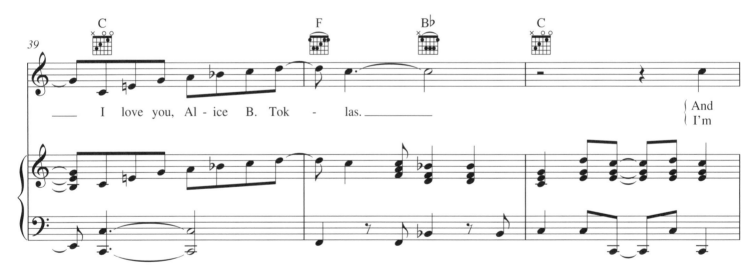

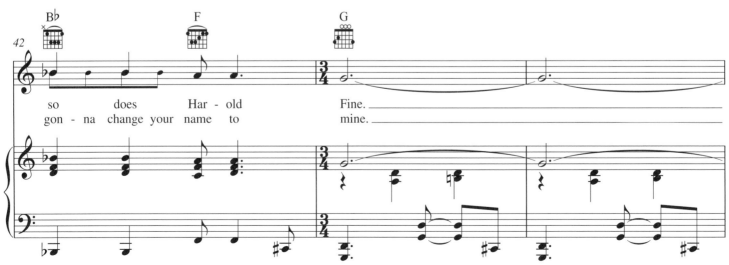

Waltz with the fur-ry fish-es, cur-ried
Kiss lime and lem-on la-dies, ice cream

dish-es, sil-ly ti-gers wear-ing but-ter-flies fly-ing fur-ther than
la-dies, Or-phan An-nie, Er-nest Hem-ing-way strum-ming Bon-nie's gui-

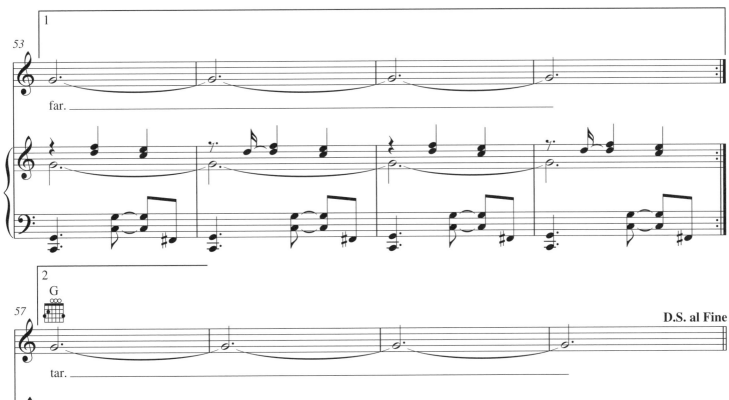

far.

tar.

LOVE AND AMBITION
from the 1956 Film THE TEN COMMANDMENTS

By ELMER BERNSTEIN

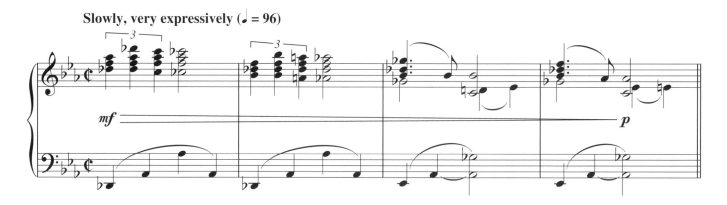

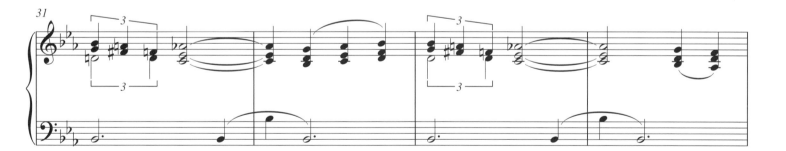

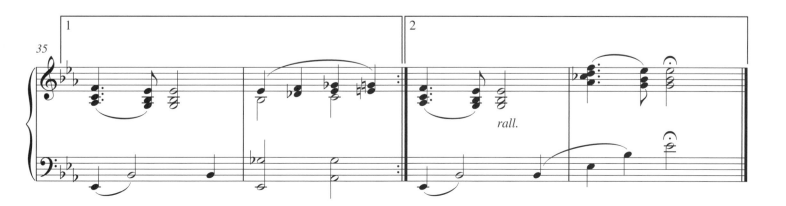

LOVE ME TRUE

from the 1966 Film CAST A GIANT SHADOW

Words by ERNIE SHELDON
Music by ELMER BERNSTEIN

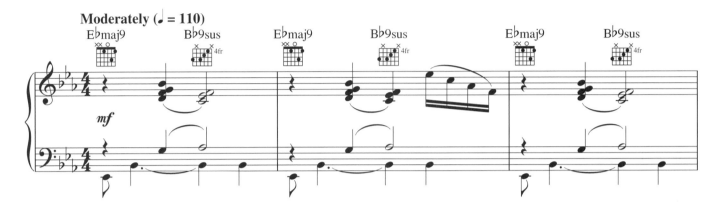

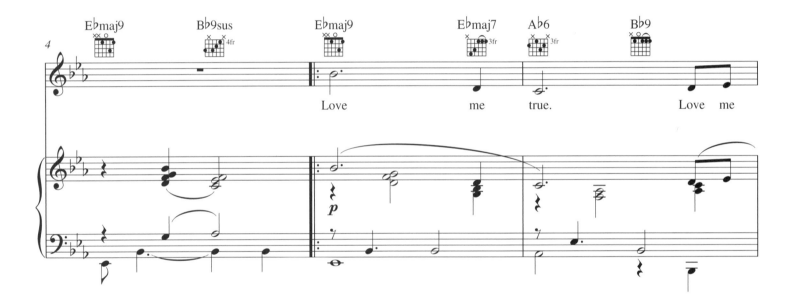

Love me true. Love me

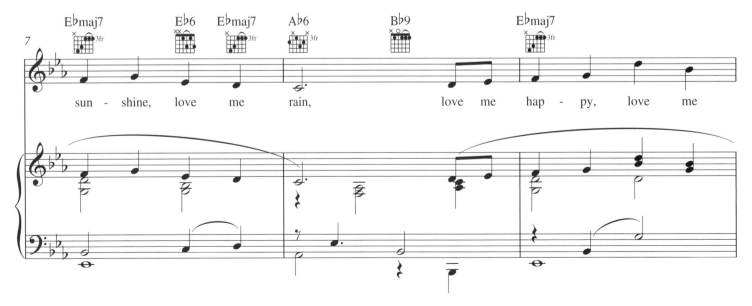

sun-shine, love me rain, love me hap-py, love me

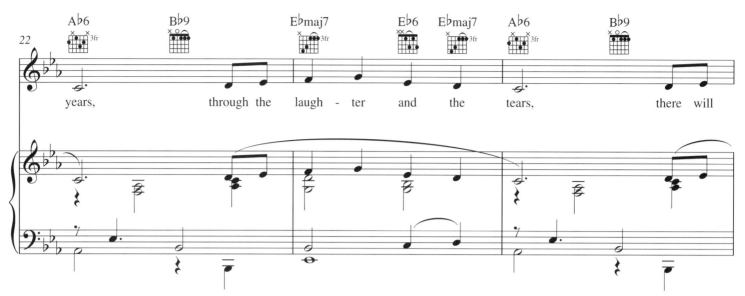

years, through the laugh - ter and the tears, there will

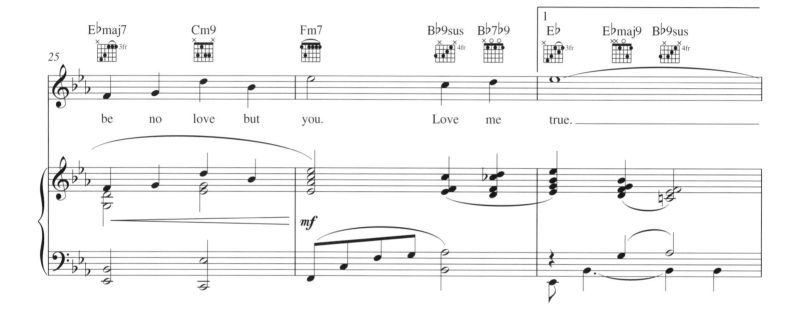

be no love but you. Love me true. _____

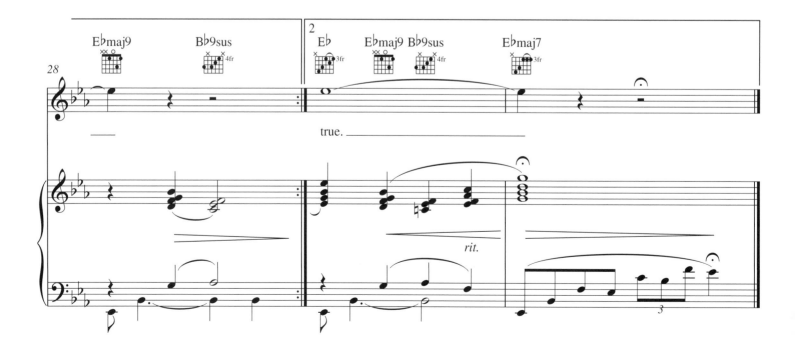

_____ true. _____

LOVE WITH THE PROPER STRANGER

from the 1963 Paramount Motion Picture LOVE WITH THE PROPER STRANGER

Words by JOHNNY MERCER
Music by ELMER BERNSTEIN

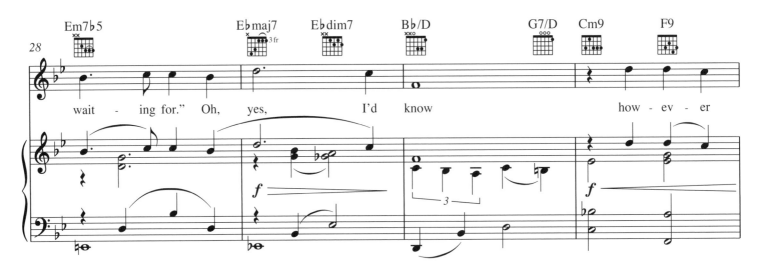

wild it seemed, you know I'd know. And I'd

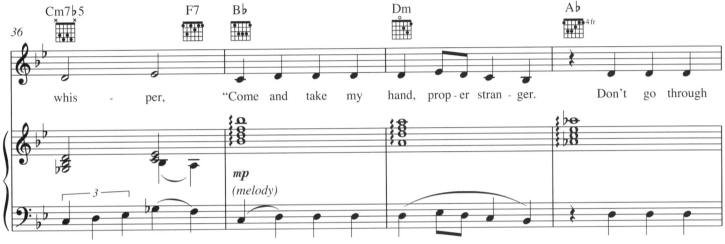

whis - per, "Come and take my hand, prop-er stran-ger. Don't go through

life as a stran - ger, for I'm a poor prop-er stran-ger, too." ____

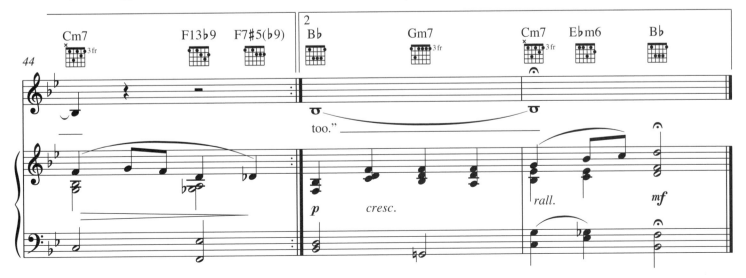

too." ____

LOVING ECHOES OF PAST TIMES

By ELMER BERNSTEIN

Editor's note: Written for Eve Bernstein on her birthday, 1988

slowing   *in tempo*

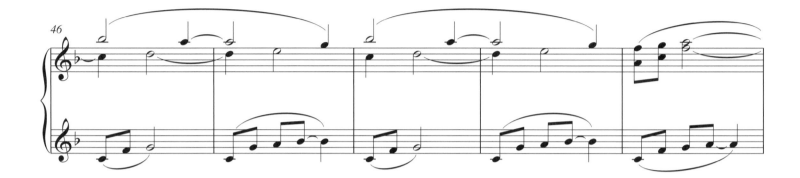

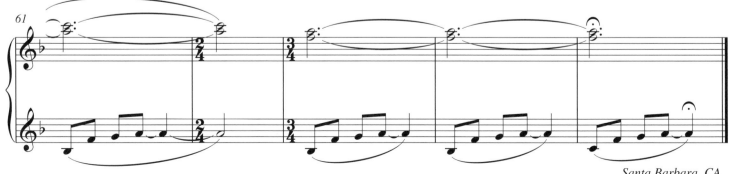

Santa Barbara, CA
August–September 1988

THE MAGNIFICENT SEVEN

from the 1960 Film THE MAGNIFICENT SEVEN

By ELMER BERNSTEIN
Piano arrangement by Patrick Russ

With gusto ($\quarternote$ = ca. 144)

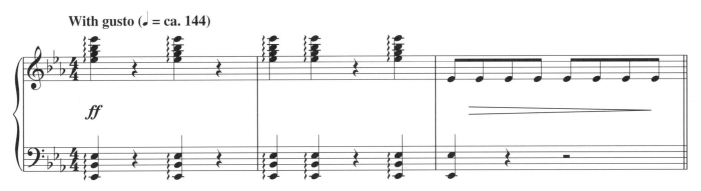

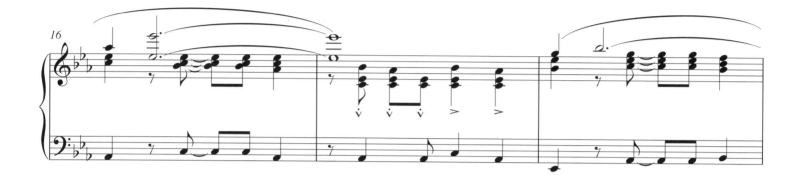

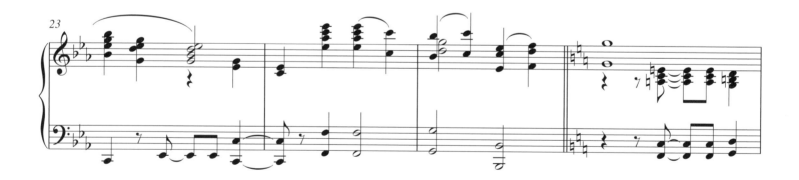

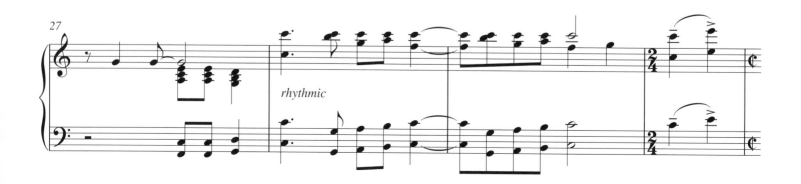

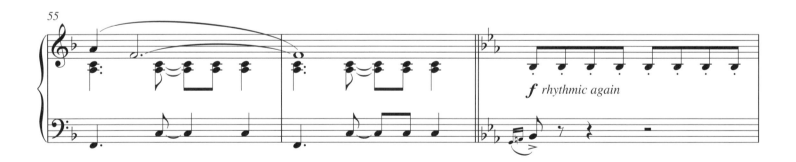

f *jubilant!*

MOLLY-O

from the 1955 Film THE MAN WITH THE GOLDEN ARM

Words by SYLVIA FINE
Music by ELMER BERNSTEIN

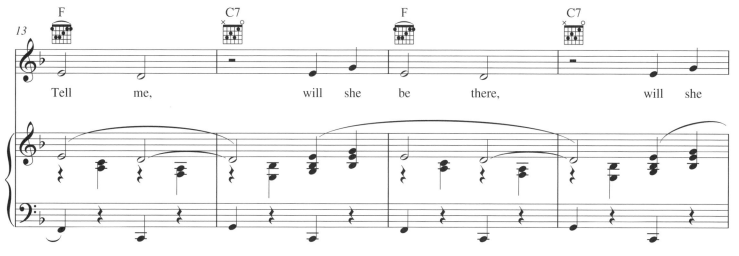

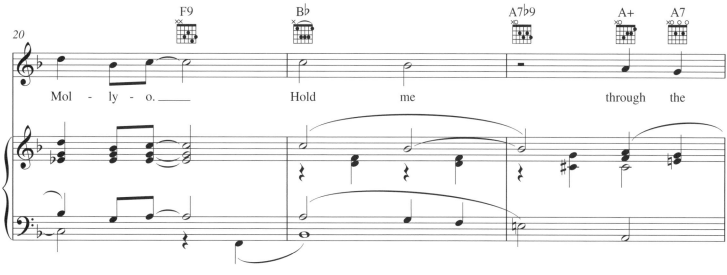

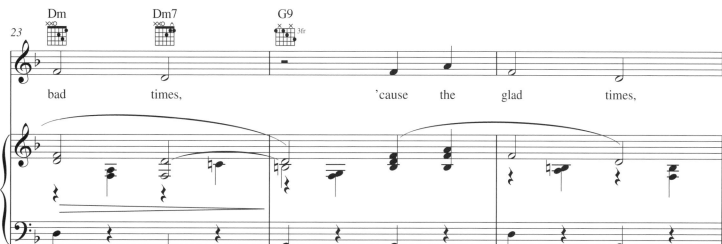

they come ___ and they go. No blues will

I mind long as I find she is

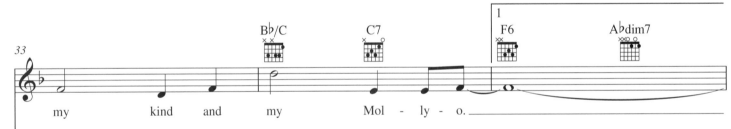

my kind and my Mol - ly - o. _____

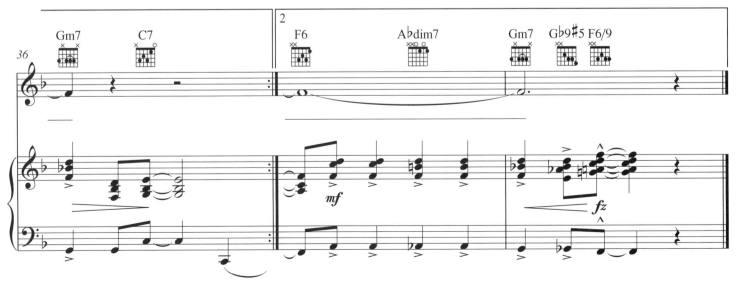

MONICA

from the 1964 Motion Picture THE CARPETBAGGERS

Words by EARL SHUMAN
Music by ELMER BERNSTEIN

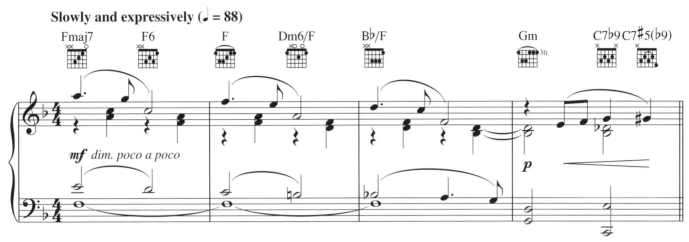

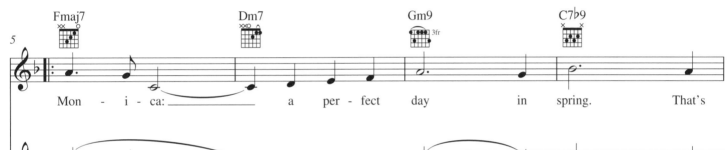

Mon - i - ca: _____ a per - fect day in spring. That's

Mon - i - ca, _____ the dream that rain - bows bring.

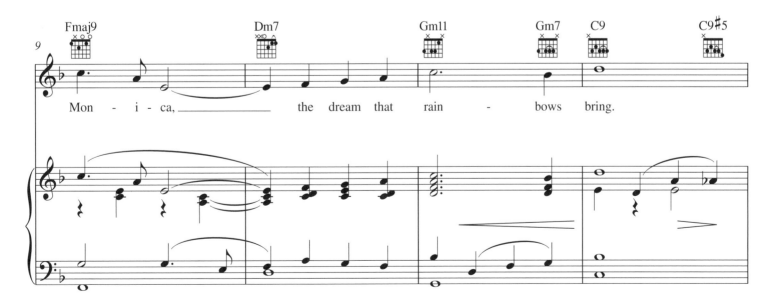

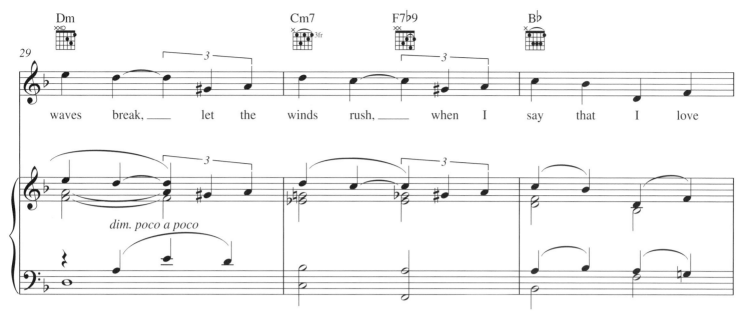

waves break, ___ let the winds rush, ___ when I say that I love

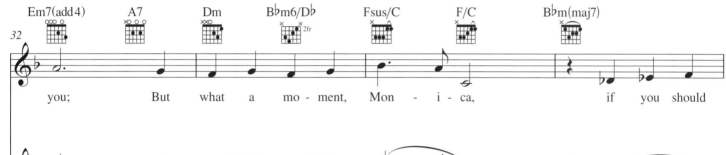

you; But what a mo-ment, Mon-i-ca, if you should

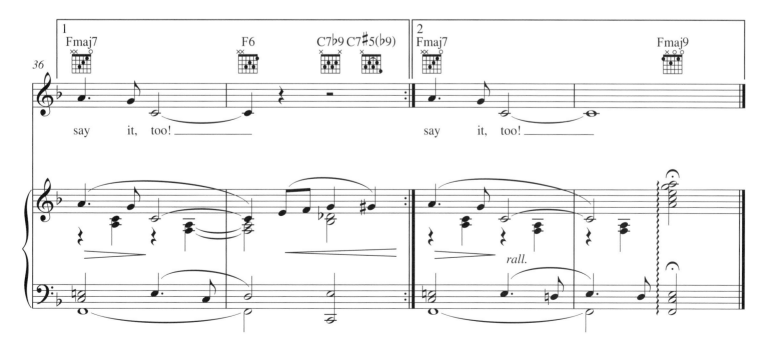

say it, too! ___ say it, too! ___

MONIQUE

from the 1958 Film KINGS GO FORTH

Words by SAMMY CAHN
Music by ELMER BERNSTEIN

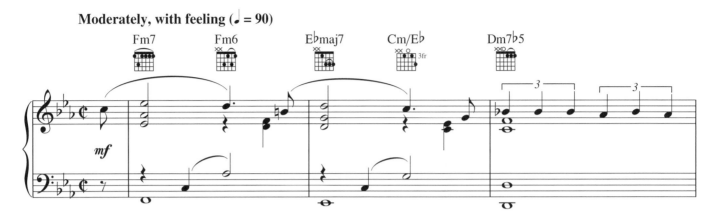

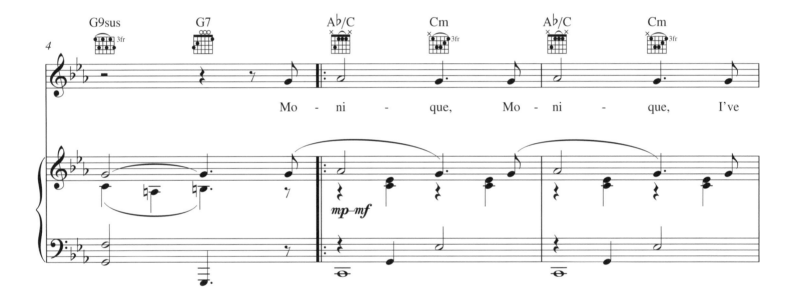

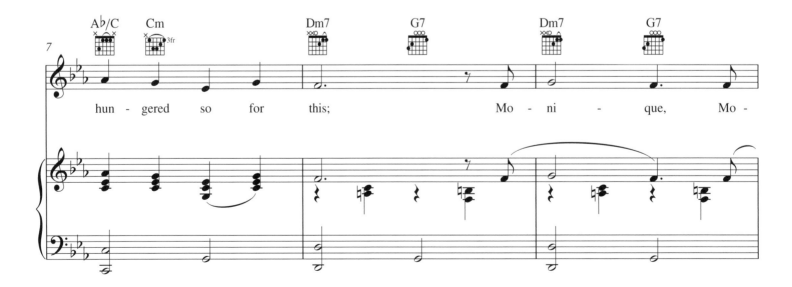

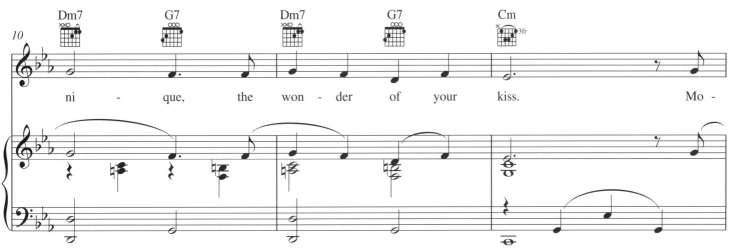

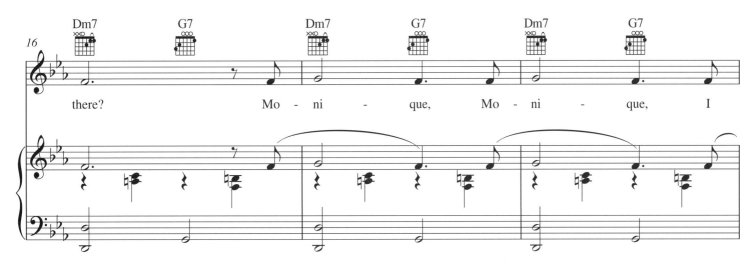

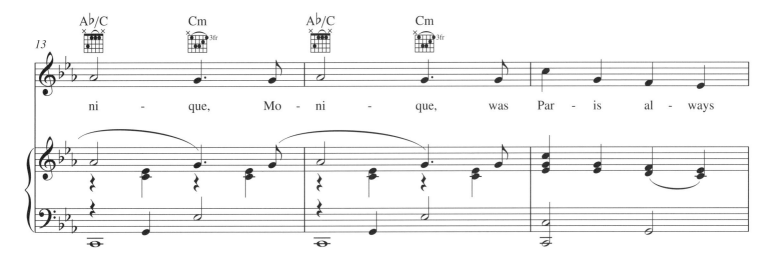

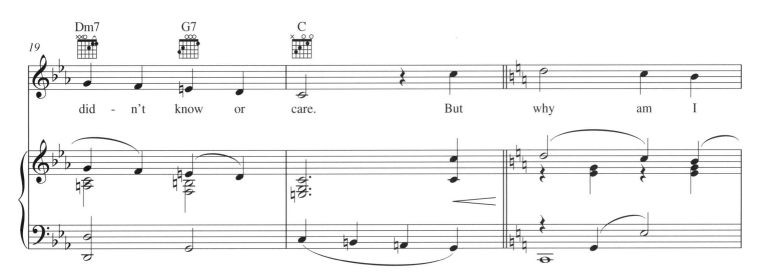

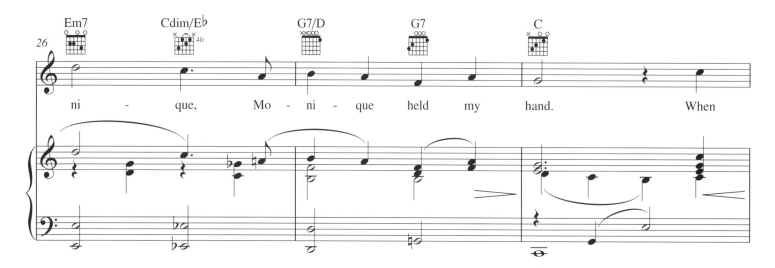

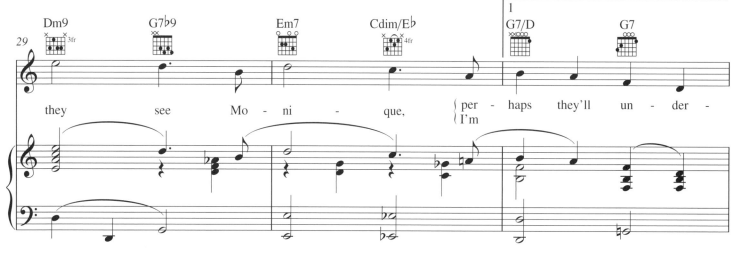

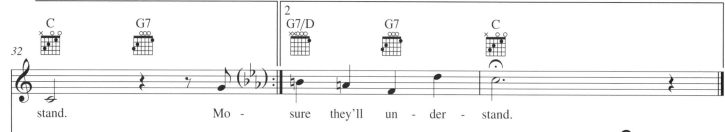

NATIONAL GEOGRAPHIC THEME

from the Television Series
(1966)

By ELMER BERNSTEIN
Piano arrangement by Patrick Russ

Bright 4 (♩ = 156)

RAT RACE - LOVE THEME

from the 1960 Film THE RAT RACE

By ELMER BERNSTEIN

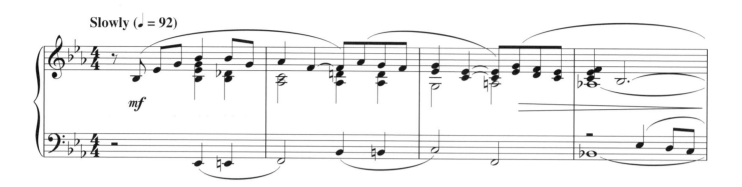

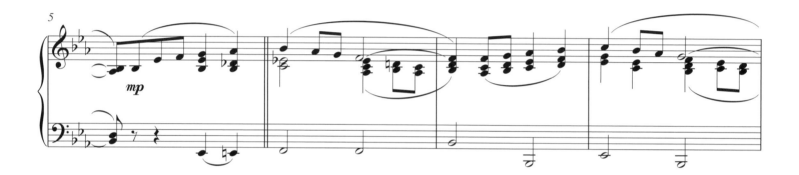

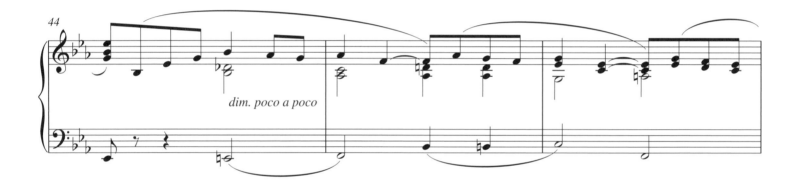

THEME FROM THE SCALPHUNTERS

from the 1968 Film THE SCALPHUNTERS

By ELMER BERNSTEIN

SIDE OF THE ANGELS

Music by ELMER BERNSTEIN
Words by NED WASHINGTON
Arranged by Paul Henning

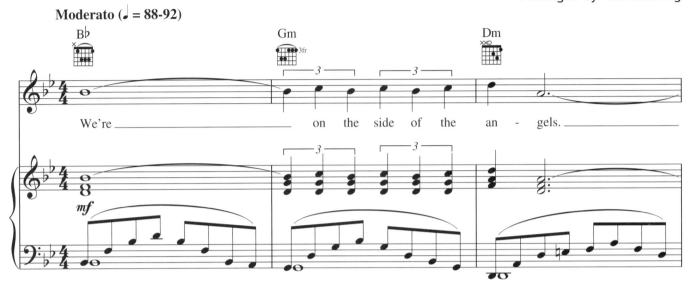

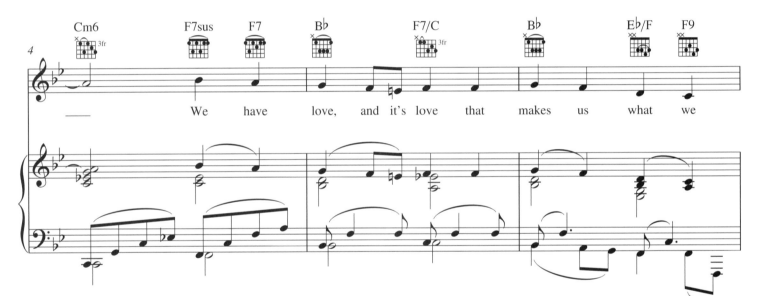

Editor's note: Based on a previously unpublished lead sheet. In early 1961 United Artists commissioned melody and lyrics for the title song of an Otto Preminger-produced film. Preminger had suggested early release of the song as a publicity vehicle, but the film was never produced.

SKY HIGH WALTZ

from the 1967 Film THOROUGHLY MODERN MILLIE

By ELMER BERNSTEIN
Piano arrangement by Patrick Russ

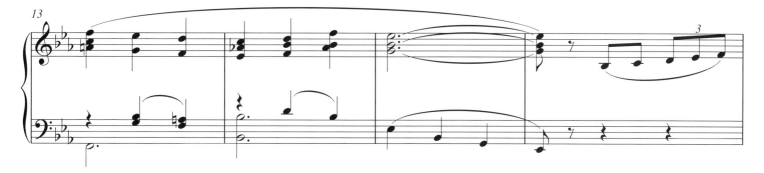

Fine

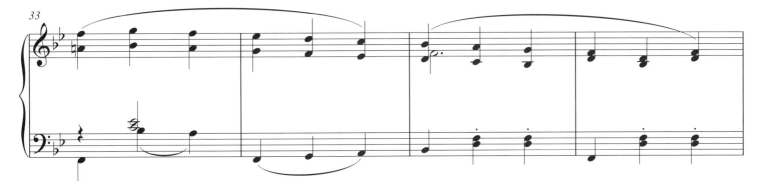

D.C. al Fine

STEP TO THE REAR

from the 1967 Broadway Musical HOW NOW, DOW JONES

Words by CAROLYN LEIGH
Music by ELMER BERNSTEIN

Editor's note: "Step to the Rear" was Hubert Humphrey's 1968 presidential campaign theme song.

Here's where we sep - a - rate the notes from the noise,___
Here's where we sep - a - rate the duck from the quack,___

___ the men from the boys,___ the rose from the
___ the ace from the pack,___ the pip from the

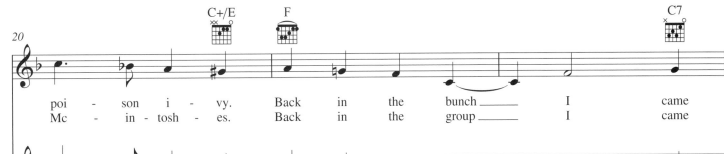

poi - son i - vy. Back in the bunch___ I came
Mc - in - tosh - es. Back in the group___ I came

up with a hunch,___ this was an up and
up with the scoop,___ this was the time to

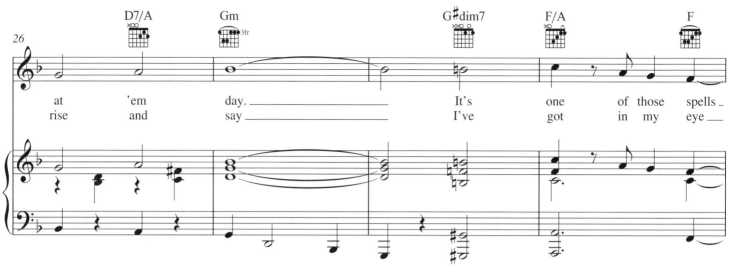

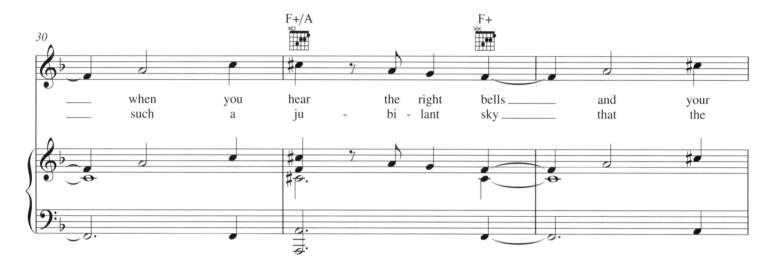

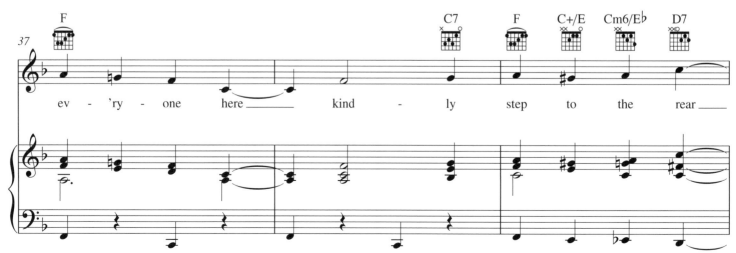

THEME FROM "STRIPES"

from the 1981 Film STRIPES

By ELMER BERNSTEIN
Piano arrangement by Patrick Russ

Tempo di marcia (♩ = ca. 120)

THAT'S ANNA
from the 1959 Film ANNA LUCASTA

Words by SAMMY CAHN
Music by ELMER BERNSTEIN

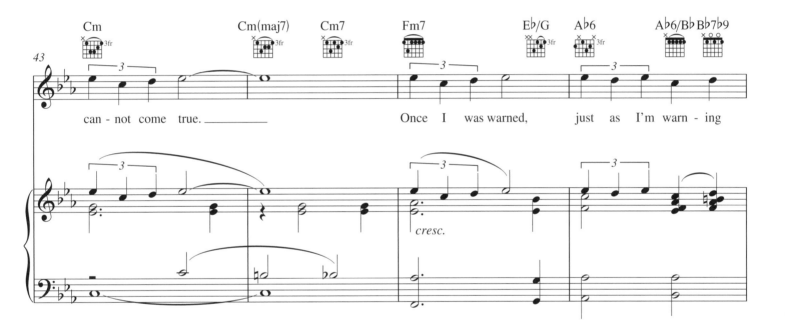

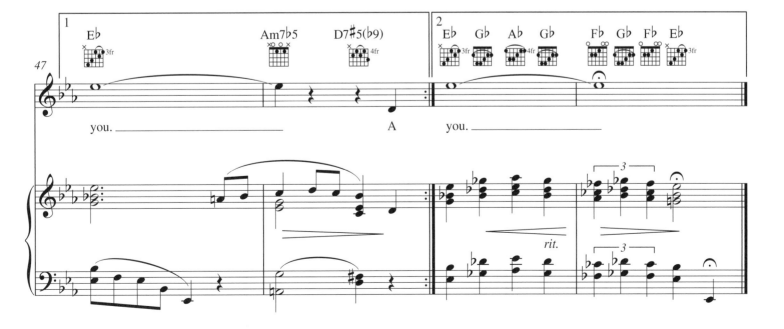

TO KILL A MOCKINGBIRD
from the 1962 Film TO KILL A MOCKINGBIRD

Music by ELMER BERNSTEIN
1999 Piano reduction by ROY PHILLIPPE
Edited by ELMER BERNSTEIN

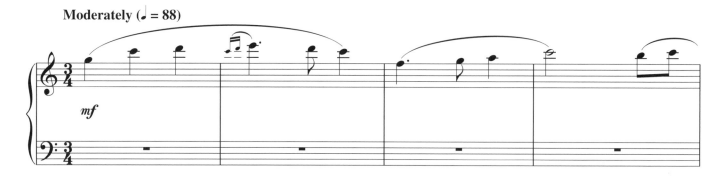

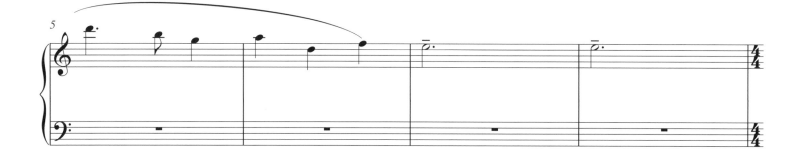

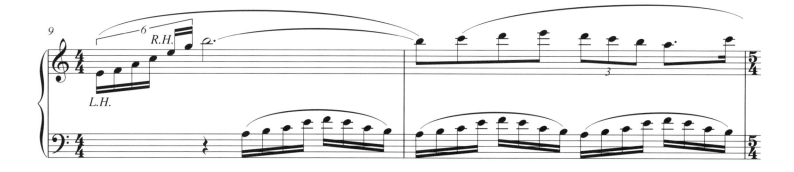

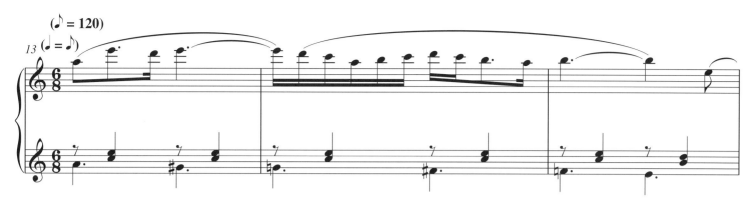

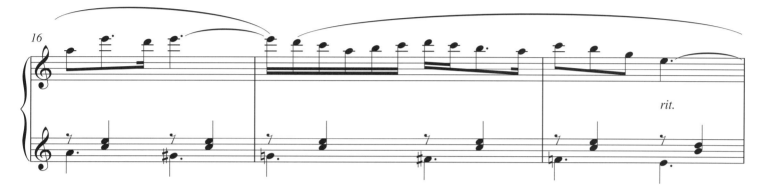

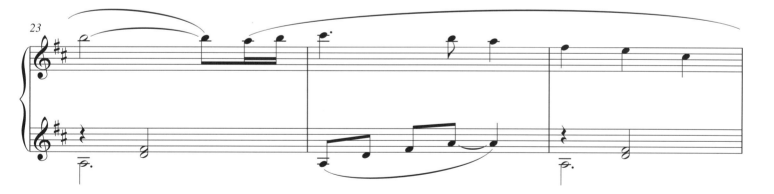

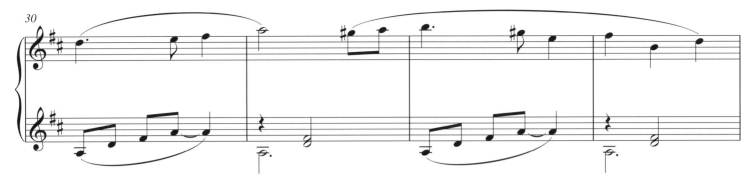

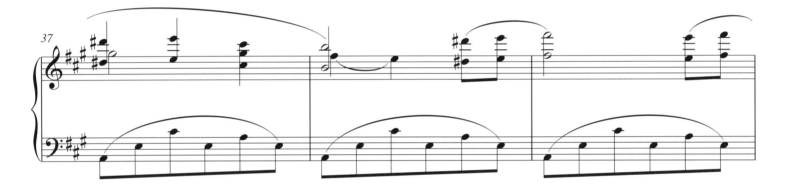

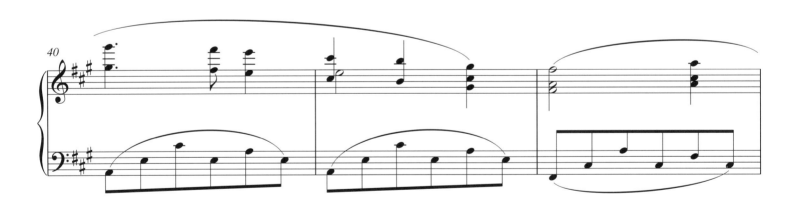

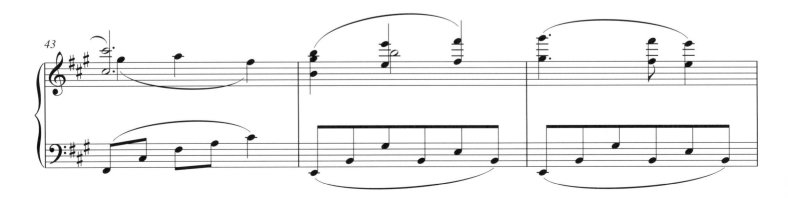

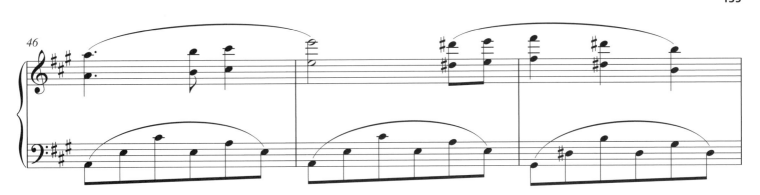

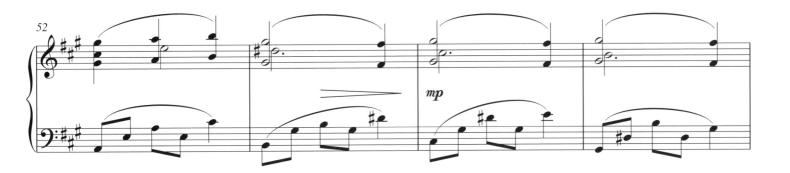

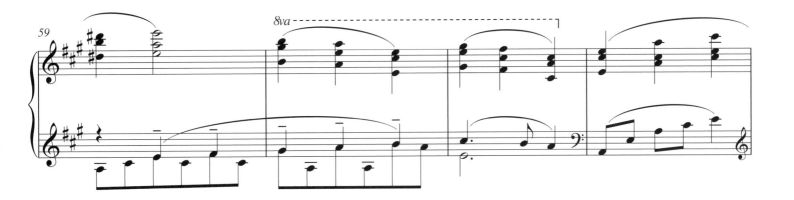

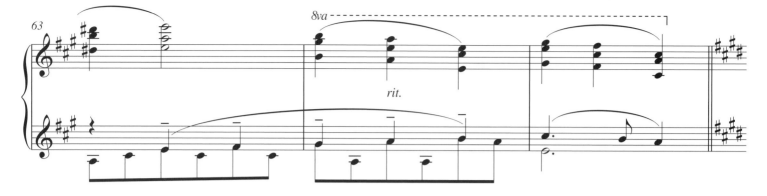

TO KILL A MOCKINGBIRD

from the 1962 Film TO KILL A MOCKINGBIRD

for Emilie, on her 10th birthday

Music by ELMER BERNSTEIN
Children's Piano Solo arrangement by Elmer Bernstein

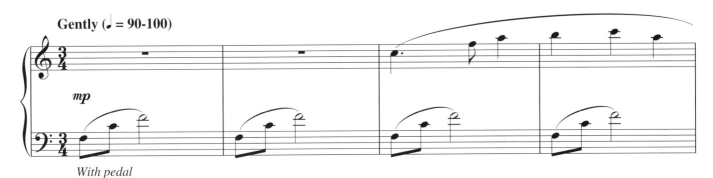

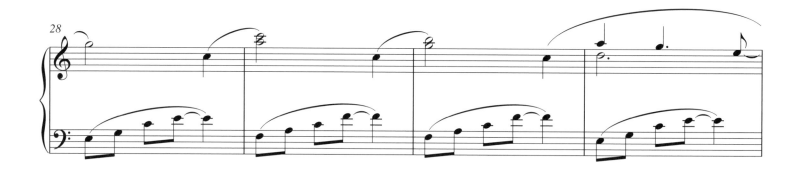

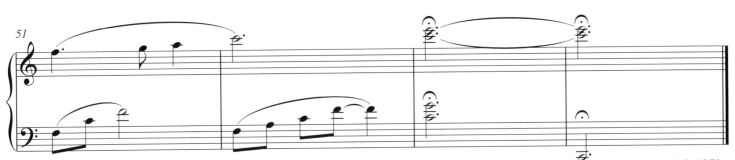

July 3, 1979

TRUE GRIT
Theme from the 1969 Paramount Picture TRUE GRIT

Words by DON BLACK
Music by ELMER BERNSTEIN

One day, lit - tle girl, the sad - ness will

leave your face _____ as soon as we've

won your fight to get jus - tice done.

WALK AWAY
from the 1967 Broadway Musical HOW NOW, DOW JONES

Music by ELMER BERNSTEIN
Words by CAROLYN LEIGH

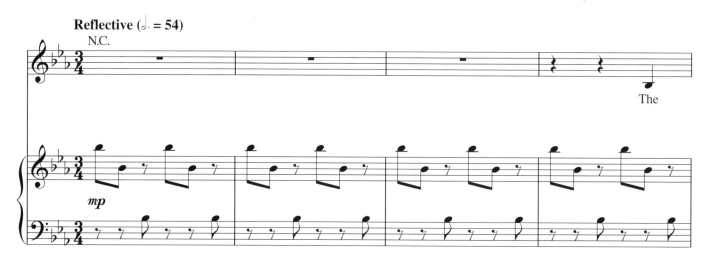

night the world was your pas - try shop, to -

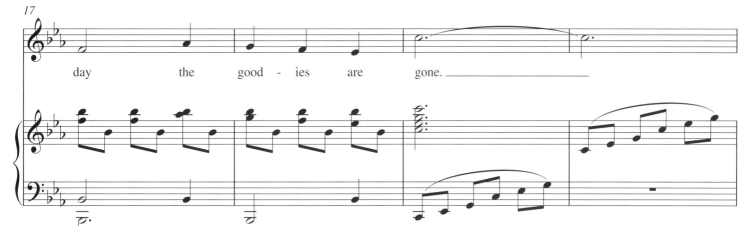

day the good - ies are gone.

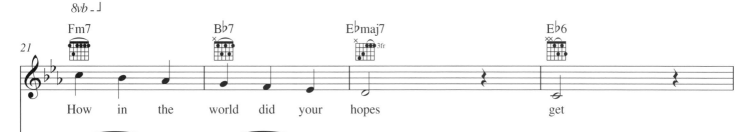

Fm7   B♭7   E♭maj7   E♭6

How in the world did your hopes get

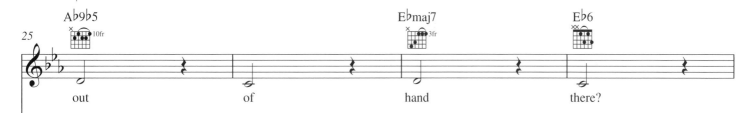

A♭9♭5   E♭maj7   E♭6

out of hand there?

Stronger, but still fancy free

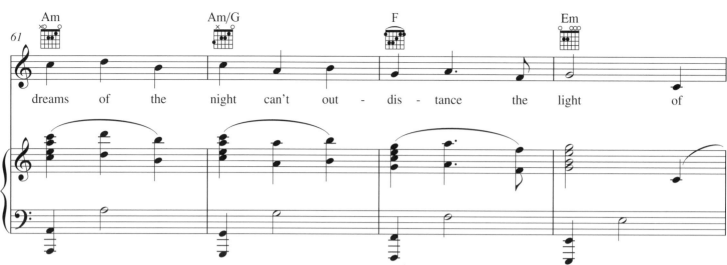

dreams of the night can't out - dis - tance the light of

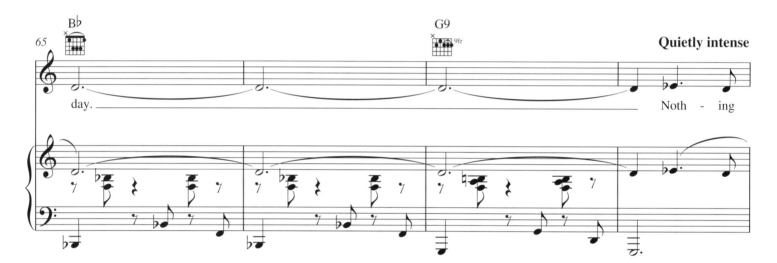

day. _____ Noth - ing

Quietly intense

lost, noth - ing ow - ing. _____ It was

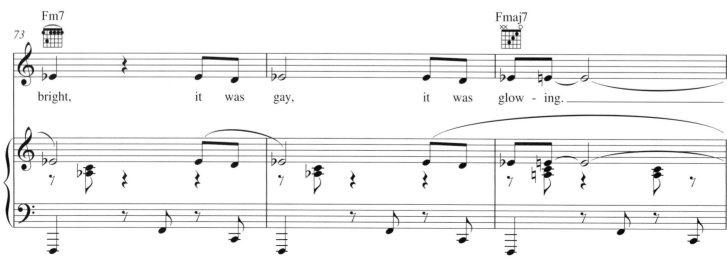

bright, it was gay, it was glow - ing. _____

150

WALK ON THE WILD SIDE

from the 1962 Film WALK ON THE WILD SIDE

Words by MACK DAVID
Music by ELMER BERNSTEIN

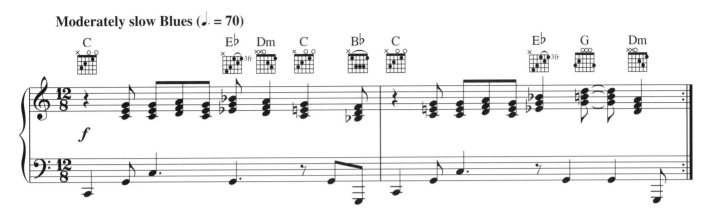

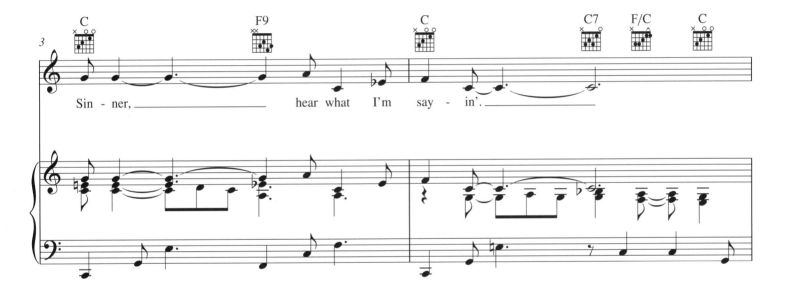

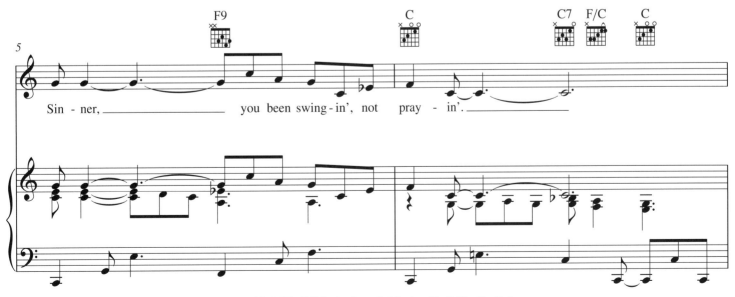

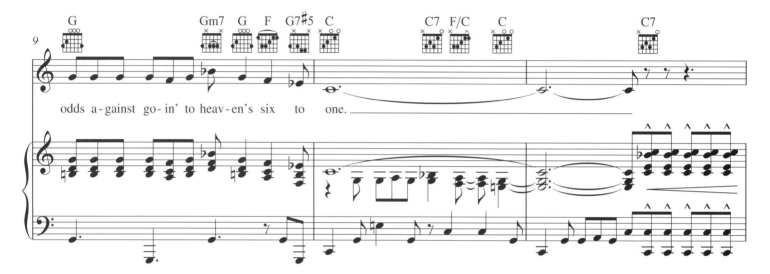

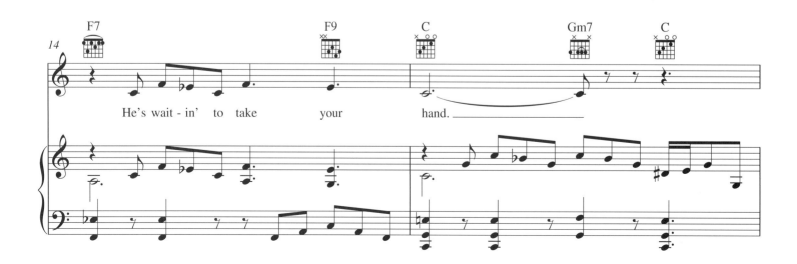

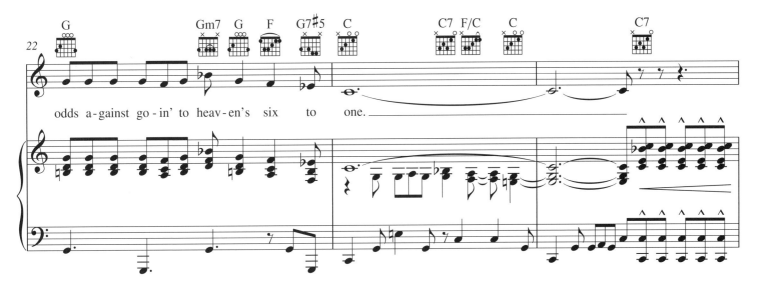

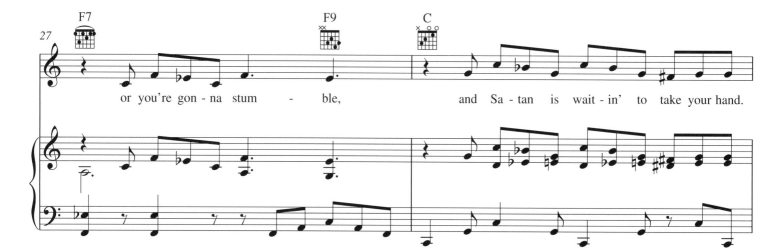

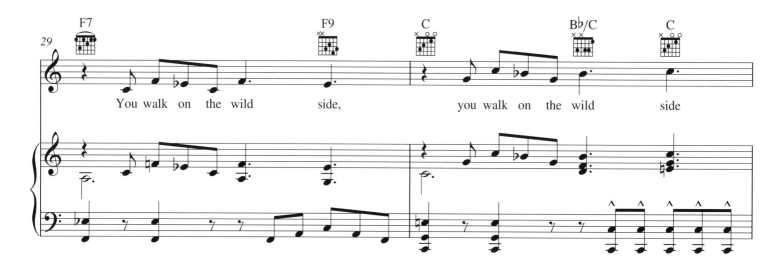

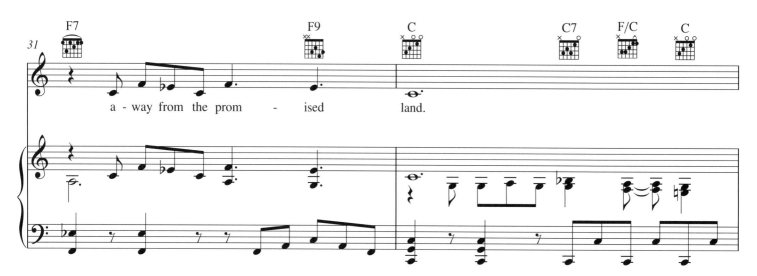

One day of pray - in' and six___ nights of fun,___ the

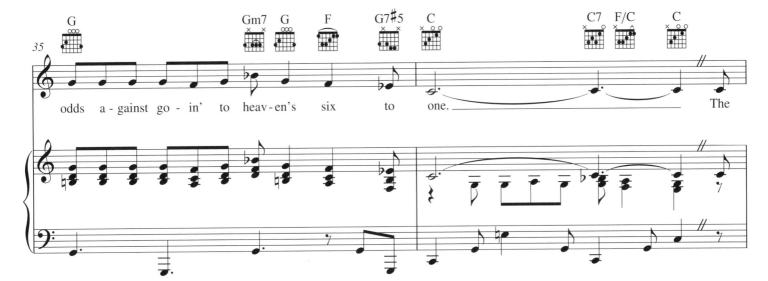

odds a - gainst go - in' to heav - en's six to one.___ The

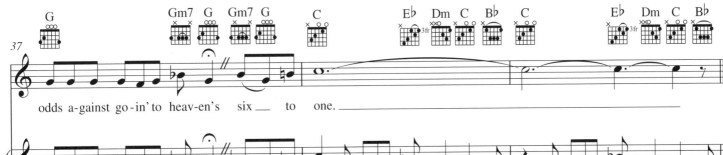

odds a-gainst go-in' to heav-en's six___ to one.___

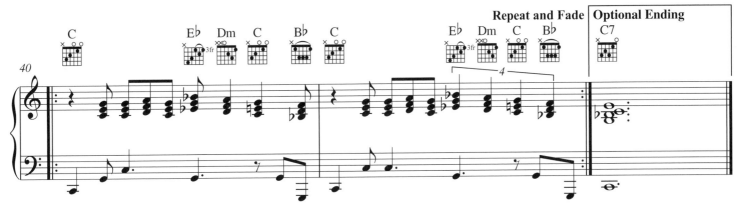

WHEREVER LOVE TAKES ME

from the 1974 Film GOLD

Music by ELMER BERNSTEIN
Words by DONALD BLACK
Arranged by Patrick Russ

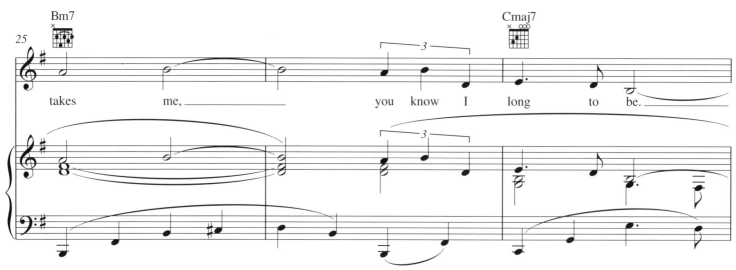

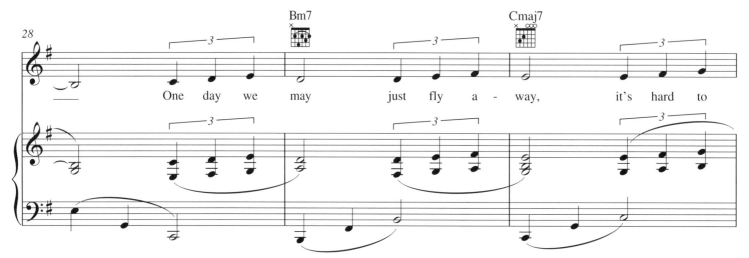

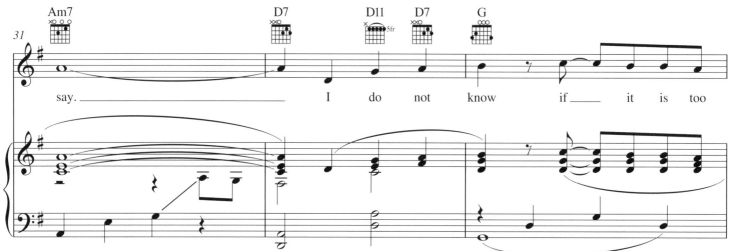